Better Reading
SPANISH

Better Reading SPANISH

A Reader and Guide to Improving Your Understanding of Written Spanish

Jean Yates

New York Chicago San Francisco Lisbon London Madrid Mexico City
Milan New Delhi San Juan Seoul Singapore Sydney Toronto

The McGraw·Hill Companies

Library of Congress Cataloging-in-Publication Data

Yates, Jean.
Better reading Spanish / Jean Yates.
p. cm. — (Better reading language series)
Includes bibliographical references.
ISBN 0-07-139137-1
1. Spanish language—Readers. I. Title. II. Series.

PC4117 .Y38 2002
468.6'421—dc21 2002035770

Copyright credits can be found in the Acknowledgments section on page 243, which is to be considered an extension of this copyright page.

7 8 9 10 11 12 13 14 15 16 17 18 19 20 21 22 23 24 DOC/DOC 0 9 8 7

ISBN-13: 978-0-07-139137-5
ISBN-10: 0-07-139137-1

McGraw-Hill books are available at special quantity discounts to use as premiums and sales promotions, or for use in corporate training programs. For more information, please write to the Director of Special Sales, Professional Publishing, McGraw-Hill, Two Penn Plaza, New York, NY 10121-2298. Or contact your local bookstore.

Other titles in the Better Reading series:

Better Reading French, Annie Heminway
Better Reading Italian, Daniela Gobetti

This book is printed on acid-free paper.

Contents

La cocina

La música

Los deportes

El cine y el teatro

El arte

La familia

El estilo de vida hoy

La historia y la política

Preface

Better Reading Spanish has been developed for English speakers who have a basic to intermediate knowledge of Spanish and is designed to help them read Spanish better and to encourage them to read more.

To read better, we must read more. As an encouragement for beginning readers, I have organized this book according to eight areas of interest: cuisine, music, sports, cinema/theater, art, family, contemporary lifestyles, and history/politics. At least one of these areas should interest the reader immediately, and after that subject is explored, interest in another will follow.

The selections include material that has appeared in newspapers, magazines, books, brochures, and flyers, as well as on the Internet. In addition to recipes, essays, poems, book excerpts, and songs, there are original articles appearing in print for the first time. Selections not otherwise credited were compiled, adapted, or created by the author. While each section's material relates to a topic in Hispanic culture, the section as a whole is not intended to be an overview or summary of the topic. Instead, the selections have been chosen for their broad appeal, their variety, and their likelihood to inspire readers to explore new horizons and to feel confident as they encounter the written word in Spanish in its myriad forms.

Each section begins with selections that are easiest to read, although none of the material has been simplified. The selections become progressively more difficult within each section, and each section ends with a selection written by a contemporary Spanish or Latin-American author who has received critical literary acclaim. Each reading selection is followed by one or more exercises designed to help readers develop skills in understanding what they are reading. The overall goal is to help readers develop reading strategies that will help them understand and benefit from future reading material. If we can read better, we will read more.

How to use this book

One of the joys of reading is that you can read what you want, when you want, however you want.

The format of *Better Reading Spanish* enables you to use, and benefit from, the book in different ways. One approach is to select a topic that interests you, read each of the selections in order, writing the exercises after each one, until you have completed the final, most difficult selection. If you are really interested in this topic, you will probably be able to read the final selection—because you want to and because you have been developing important reading skills that make the material easier to read. Then you may choose another topic that interests you.

A second approach is to read the first, easiest selection in each section, writing the exercises as you go, then progress to the second selection of each section, and so on until you have completed the most difficult selections in the book.

In your approach to an individual selection, first read it in its entirety, then proceed with the exercises, which are designed to help you read without the aid of a dictionary. The exercises encourage development of the following skills.

- *Skimming for general meaning*: reading the entire selection quickly to determine its general purpose and content
- *Scanning for details*: noting headings, references, and other guides to quick information
- *Using word formation to determine meaning*: knowing how prefixes, suffixes, verb endings, and grammatical forms indicate meaning
- *Using cognates to determine meaning*: comparing Spanish words with related words in English
- *Using context to determine meaning*: making educated guesses about the meaning of unfamiliar words by determining their role in the context of a sentence, paragraph, or entire selection
- *Learning idioms and other expressions*: recognizing and learning the meaning of forms that cannot be translated literally
- *Understanding artistic expression*: recognizing literary devices that authors use
- *Rereading for comprehension*: reading an entire selection again to gain greater understanding

Using a dictionary

Looking up every unfamiliar word in a dictionary is tiresome and slows you down, thereby detracting from the pleasure of reading. I suggest the following approach to using a dictionary while reading this book.

- Complete all the exercises for a selection before consulting a dictionary.
- Don't worry if you don't understand every single word; read to get the overall meaning. A rule of thumb is that you look up a word only after you have stumbled over it in three different places.
- Consult a Spanish-Spanish dictionary first: It will give you a broader understanding of how the language works. Keep this dictionary nearby.
- Use a Spanish-English dictionary only as a last resort. Put it in a hard-to-reach place.

La cocina

Guía para la buena alimentación

GUÍA PARA LA BUENA ALIMENTACIÓN

Cómo alimentarse para mantener la buena salud:

1. *Coma alimentos de los cinco grupos alimenticios todos los días.*
2. *Coma diferentes alimentos de cada grupo cada día.*

Todos los días coma:	*Las porciones que se recomiendan*				
Del grupo de la LECHE *para el calcio* *2 a 4 porciones*	 Leche 1 taza	Queso 1½ a 2 onzas	Yogur 1 taza	Café con leche 1 taza	Helados de crema o leche, yogur congelado ½ taza
Del grupo de la CARNE *para el hierro* *2 a 3 porciones*	 Carne cocida, sin grasa 2 a 3 onzas	Pollo y pavo cocidos 2 a 3 onzas	Huevo 1	Chícharos y frijoles secos y cocinados ½ taza	Pescado magro cocido 2 a 3 onzas
Del grupo de las VERDURAS/ VEGETALES *para la vitamina A* *3 a 5 porciones*	 Verduras/vegetales frescos ½ taza	Tomate, papa 1 mediano	Verduras/vegetales de hojas frescas 1 taza	Verduras/vegetales cocidos ½ taza	Plátanos de cocinar ½ mediano
Del grupo de las FRUTAS *para la vitamina C* *2 a 4 porciones*	 Jugo ¾ taza	Frutas frescas, enlatadas o cocidas ½ taza	Mango, manzana, guineo/plátano, naranja/china 1 mediana	Papaya ½	Uvas 10 a 12
Del grupo de los GRANOS *para la fibra* *6 a 11 porciones*	 Pan 1 rebanada	Arroz, pasta ½ taza	Cereal cocido ½ taza	Pan de hamburguesa, muffin ½	Tortilla, panecito 1

Adaptada del National Dairy Council®, 1993.

MÉXICO

Menú de México

Casa Paco

Oaxaca

Entradas frías y calientes	pesos
Quesadillas tradicionales	60
Canasta de chapulines	65
Brocheta de quesos	55
Camarones con aguacate	120
Ensaladas	
De frutas	50
De jitomate*	60
De pollo	65
De jamón, pollo y queso	90
Sopas	
De elote	40
Sabina (con flor de calabaza y hongos)*	40
Lentejas con plátano frito	40
Sopa del día	40
Pescados y mariscos	
Filete de pescado almendrado	135
Camarones rellenos	180
Medallón de camarones (con arroz y verduras)	180
Filete de pescado en hoja de plátano*	150
Rincón oaxaqueño	
Pollo en mole negro	75
Dos tamales oaxaqueños	55
Tacos de pollo	65
Pechuga de pollo rellena de huitlacoche	90
Enmoladas de pollo	65

Aves y carnes

Suprema de pollo a la manzana	75
Mignon de filete de res	160
Carne asada a la tampiqueña (servida con arroz, guacamole, rajas y enmolada)	150

Sandwiches

Hamburguesa de res (servida con papas fritas y ensalada de col)	80
Sándwich de jamón y queso	60
Pepito tradicional (de filete de res con papas fritas y guacamole)	90

Para los niños

Consomé de pollo (con arroz y pollo)	30
Spaghetti al gusto	65
Tacos de carne picada	65
Fajitas de pollo	60

Postres

Selección diaria de postres de la casa	35
Helados y nieves	30

Bebidas

Té	16
Chocolate caliente y frío	20
Café americano	15
Expresso	20
Capuccino	25

Pregunte por nuestra selección de vinos.

Si usted desea algo especial no mencionado en el menú, nuestro capitán hará lo posible para satisfacer su gusto.

* Bajo en calorías

EJERCICIOS

SCANNING FOR INFORMATION

A Refer to the *Guía para la buena alimentación* and complete the following sentences.

1 *La manzana, el plátano y la naranja* belong to the group of *las* ____________.

2 *Las verduras* are a good source of *la vitamina* ____________.

3 *El queso, el yogur y el helado* belong to the group of *la* ____________ and are a good source of *el* ____________.

4 Good sources of *hierro* are found in the group of *la* ____________, which includes ____________, ____________, ____________, ____________ *y* ____________.

5 *El pan, el arroz y el cereal* are examples of sources of *la* ____________.

B Refer to the *menú de México* and answer the following questions.

1 *El helado* and *la nieve* are choices in which menu category?

____

2 In what courses could you get a serving of *el pollo*?

____________ ____________

____________ ____________

____________ ____________

____________ ____________

____________ ____________

3 What types of *café* are offered?

____________ ____________

____

4 What does an asterisk (*) next to a menu item mean?

____

5 What is the cheapest item on the menu? ____________

6 What are the most expensive?

____________ ____________

7 Is wine offered? ____________

C Refer to the *Guía para la buena alimentación* and the *menú de México* and answer the following questions.

1 What could you order to provide *el hierro* for a child?

______________________ ______________________

____

2 Which items on the menu are a good source of *la fibra*? (Write as many items as you can.)

____

____

____

3 What would you order as a source of *la vitamina C*?

______________________ ______________________

Gazpacho

Número de personas 6

Tiempo de preparación 15 minutos

Ingredientes

1¼ kg de tomates bien maduros, pelados y sin semillas
½ cebolla
1 pepino pequeño
1 pimiento verde pequeño
200 g de miga de pan (del día anterior y remojada en agua)
1 taza de aceite fino
2 cucharadas soperas de vinagre
unos trozos de hielo
sal

Elaboración

Ponga en la batidora, en unas cuantas veces, las hortalizas, un poco de vinagre, un poco de aceite y parte del pan. Bata bien hasta que quede muy fino. Póngalo en la sopera y métala en la nevera hasta el momento de servirlo. Debe tomarse bien fresco.

Cuando lo vaya a servir, póngale unos cubitos de hielo y muévalo para enfriarlo bien. Aparte, sirva las verduras picaditas por separado, para que cada uno se las sirva a su gusto.

EJERCICIOS

USING COGNATES TO GUESS MEANING

Cognates are words that are similar in form and meaning in two languages.

Inés Ortega, *La cocina básica*, pp. 218–19.

A Write the English equivalent of each of the following words.

1	*número*	______	9	*anterior*	______
2	*personas*	______	10	*fino*	______
3	*tiempo*	______	11	*vinagre*	______
4	*preparación*	______	12	*sal*	______
5	*minutos*	______	13	*parte*	______
6	*ingredientes*	______	14	*momento*	______
7	*tomates*	______	15	*servir*	______
8	*maduros*	______	16	*mover*	______

B What are the two different meanings of the word *fino* in the recipe?

______ ______

USING CONTEXT TO GUESS MEANING

It is important to understand the relationships conveyed by prepositions.

C Write possible English equivalents for the following prepositions.

1	*de*	______	3	*sin*	______
2	*con*	______	4	*en*	______

Most prepositions are best learned in combination with other words, as part of phrases.

D What does *por separado* mean in English? ______

E The recipe lists *tomates, cebolla, pepino,* and *pimiento verde* as ingredients. According to the *elaboración,* in what two categories do these items belong?

______ ______

F Answer the following questions.

1 If *frío* means "cold," what does *enfriar* mean? ______

2 You put *hielo* in the gazpacho *para enfriarlo*; what is the meaning of *hielo*?

______

3 You put the gazpacho *en la nevera para enfriarlo*; what is the meaning of *nevera*? ______

USING WORD ENDINGS TO DETERMINE MEANING

A suffix (an ending added to a word or word root) often tells us the function of the word in a sentence.

-ar/-er/-ir Indicates the infinitive form of a verb, which is often used when the verb is the subject of a sentence or when it is used after a conjugated verb or after a preposition. (The infinitive form is the one used in dictionary entries.)

-ar	*cocinar*	***Cocinar*** *es divertido.* **Cooking** is fun.
-er	*comer*	*Queremos* ***comer****.* We want **to eat**.
-ir	*batir*	*Después de* ***batir*** *la crema,...* After **whipping** the cream, . . .

-ado/-ido/-to Indicates the participle form of a verb, which is used after *haber* to show that the action has already been completed.

-ado	*cocinado*	cooked
-ido	*comido*	eaten
	batido	beaten/whipped/blended

-ero/-era Changes a verb to a noun, sometimes used to indicate a person who performs the action indicated.

-ero	*el cocinero*	the male cook
-era	*la cocinera*	the female cook

This suffix can also change a noun to another noun, one that indicates a receptacle for the original noun.

la sopa	+ *-era* →	*la sopera*
the soup		the soup tureen

-dor/-dora Changes a verb to a noun, sometimes used to indicate the person or thing that performs the action indicated.

-dora	*la batidora*	the blender

This suffix can also indicate a place where an action occurs.

-dor	*el comedor*	the dining room

La cocina may refer not only to the room where food is prepared, but also to the "cuisine" of a particular area.

G Write the English meaning of the following words and phrases.

______________	______________	______________
El cocinero	*cocina*	*la cocina mexicana*

______________.
en la cocina.

The participle of a verb may also be used as an adjective to describe a noun.

congelar	to freeze
verduras ***congeladas***	**frozen** vegetables

H Using the participle form of the verb on the left, complete each Spanish phrase, then write its English meaning on the line below. Remember that an adjective always agrees in gender and number with the noun it describes.

1 *pelar* to peel *los tomates* ______________
____

2 *mojar* to moisten *el pan* ______________
____

3 *cocinar* to cook *las verduras* ______________
____

4 *batir* to beat *los huevos* ______________
____

5 *cocer* to stew *las frutas* ______________
____

6 *asar* to grill *la carne* ______________
____

7 *hervir* to boil *el agua* ______________
____

The suffixes *-ante/-ente/-iente* can also change a verb into an adjective.

calentar (ie)	to heat
caliente	hot

I Write the English meaning of the following phrases.

1 *picar* to bite/sting/cut *comida picante* ______________
2 *hervir (ie)* to boil *agua hirviente* ______________

Bien after a verb usually means "in a satisfactory way." *Bien* before an adjective usually means "very."

Marta cocina ***bien***.	Marta cooks **well**.
La comida está ***bien*** *picante*.	The food is **very** spicy.

J Write the English meaning of the following sentences.

1 *Los niños comen bien.*

____

2 *La sopa está bien fría.*

____

3 *La comida está bien caliente.*

____

The prefix *re-* before a verb often means "again." *Re-* before an adjective, including a participle used as an adjective, usually means "excessively."

K Write the English meaning of the following phrases.

1 *pan remojado* ______________

2 *frijoles refritos* ______________

3 *recalentar la sopa* ______________

L Complete the following sentences by writing the English equivalent of the Spanish words and phrases.

1 The *tomates* should be *maduros*, ______________ (*pelados*) and *sin* ______________ (*semillas*). The ______________ (*pan*) is from ______________ (*el día anterior*), and it is broken up into ______________ (*migas*), which have been ______________ (*remojadas en agua*). La *sopa* is served from a ______________ (*sopera*).

2 Since the *gazpacho* is served ______________ (*muy frío*), it is put into the ______________ (*nevera*) until ready to serve. To keep it cold, you add ______________ (*trozos*) of ______________ (*hielo*) ______________ (*al último minuto*).

READING DIRECTIONS IN SPANISH

The directions in this recipe (and throughout this particular cookbook) are given with verbs in the command form. Directions can also be given with verbs in the infinitive form, as in the recipe for *Pastel de piña* on page 15.

M Write the infinitive form of each of the verbs that give directions in the recipe.

1 *ponga* ________________ 4 *mueva* ________________

2 *bata* ________________ 5 *sirva* ________________

3 *meta* ________________

Another common way of giving directions is to use *se* + the third-person form of the verb. The verb is singular when followed by a singular noun, and plural when followed by a plural noun.

se corta el tomate
se cortan los tomates

N Write the following directions using the *se* construction.

1 *poner las hortalizas en la batidora*

____

2 *batir la mezcla*

____

3 *meter la mezcla en la nevera*

____

4 *poner unos cubitos de hielo en el gazpacho*

____

5 *mover el gazpacho*

____

6 *servir el gazpacho*

____

Piña

Ananás (*Ananas sativus*)

Por un error garrafal la llamamos piña. Su verdadero nombre lo olvidamos hace más de cinco siglos en la salvaje confusión que fue la conquista de América. Se llamaba *ananás*, que en el lenguaje guaraní y en su sitio de origen significa "fruta exquisita". Para los pueblos precolombinos esta fragante fruta era parte de la vida diaria y del paisaje; la cultivaban cuidadosamente en hileras en sus jardines y heredades, conocían sus poderes medicinales, preparaban vino y chicha con ella y acompañaban a los muertos en sus largos viajes a la eternidad.

Cuando Colón llegó al Nuevo Mundo, los nativos se la ofrecieron como gesto de bienvenida y hospitalidad; a los españoles se les pareció a la bellota del pino europeo y, como venían en ánimo de bautizar todo lo que tenían por delante, la llamaron piña.

El descubrimiento de América provocó una febril búsqueda de tesoros y parte del botín fueron sus animales y plantas. «Estas cosas de la Nueva Castilla son en sí tan grandes e tan apartadas e tan nuevas y tan importantes e tan desviadas y peregrinas», le escribía el cronista Gonzalo Fernández de Oviedo a su rey. «La piña es una de las más hermosas fructas que yo he visto en todo el mundo que he andado. Da holgura a la vista, suavidad de olor, gusto de excelente sabor y entre todas las fructas la que mejor huele y que mejor sabor tiene. Esta fructa despierta el apetito, pero tiene un problema, que el vino bebido tras la piña no sabe bien».

La piña fue llevada a España como testimonio de «esas cosas tan desviadas y peregrinas» y siendo tan placentera y sabrosa y tan fácil su dispersión y cultivo, pronto cruzó en galeones y carabelas los mares del mundo y llegó al África, a Madagascar, a China, a Java, a la India y a las Filipinas donde se propagó rápidamente. Poco se imaginaron los nativos la transformación que su fragante fruta iba a sufrir con las necesidades, la ingeniosidad y los sueños de otros pueblos.

Clara Inés Olaya, *Frutas de América tropical y subtropical, historia y usos*, pp. 64–66, 74.

Pastel de piña

2 tazas de harina de trigo
¾ de taza de mantequilla
⅓ de taza de azúcar
1 piña
½ de taza de azúcar
½ de taza de jerez

Para la base del pastel, mezclar la harina, la mantequilla y ⅓ de taza de azúcar con agua helada. Hacer una bola y extender sobre un molde. Cocinar en horno caliente a 400° por 10 minutos. Cortar la piña en trozos pequeños y cocinar a fuego lento con el jerez y la ½ taza de azúcar hasta que la piña suavice. Subir la llama y cocinar hasta espesar y dorar. Verter sobre la base del pastel y hornear. Cubrir con crema batida y servir de inmediato.

EJERCICIOS

SKIMMING FOR MEANING

A Get an overall idea of what this selection is about by making some preliminary observations, as follows.

1 What is the title of the book from which the selection is taken (and the meaning of the title in English)?

____

____

2 What is the title of the selection (and the meaning of the title in English)?

____

3 The main text is accompanied by *una* ______________ *para la preparación de* ______________.

4 Do the verb endings in the main text indicate past, present, or future time?

____

5 What do the following expressions indicate?

a *la conquista de América* ______________

b *los pueblos precolombinos* ______________

c *el Nuevo Mundo* ______________

d *los españoles* ____________________

e *el descubrimiento de América* ____________________

f *Nueva Castilla* ____________________

g *le escribía el cronista... a su rey* ____________________

B The following Spanish words have English cognates. Write the English equivalent of each word.

Nouns

1 *error* ____________

2 *animal* ____________

3 *lenguaje* ____________

4 *origen* ____________

5 *fruta* ____________

6 *parte* ____________

7 *jardín* ____________

8 *nativo* ____________

9 *gesto* ____________

10 *tesoro* ____________

11 *planta* ____________

12 *testimonio* ____________

13 *cultivo* ____________

Adjectives

1 *salvaje* ____________

2 *exquisita* ____________

3 *fragante* ____________

4 *diaria* ____________

5 *medicinal* ____________

6 *importante* ____________

Verbs

1 *acompañar* ____________

2 *ofrecer* ____________

3 *sufrir* ____________

Adverb

1 *rápidamente* ____________

USING WORD ENDINGS TO DETERMINE MEANING

C Many English nouns that end in *-tion/-sion* have cognates in Spanish that end in *-ción/-sión.* These nouns are always feminine.

1 What nouns of this type appear in this selection?

____________ ____________ ____________

2 Change the following verbs to *-ción* nouns, indicating their gender with *la*.

a *cultivar* ____________

b *preparar* ____________

c *provocar* ____________

d *propagar* ____________

e *imaginar* ____________

D Many English nouns that end in *-ity* have cognates in Spanish that end in *-dad.* These nouns are also feminine. What nouns of this type can you find in the selection?

____________ ____________ ____________

____________ ____________ ____________

E The verb endings *-ía/-ían* and *-aba/-aban* can describe what people did repeatedly or habitually in the past. What verbs in the first paragraph indicate this type of activity?

____________ ____________ ____________

____________ ____________

F What verb form is used for the directions in the recipe?

____

El cumpleaños de Frida Kahlo

Frida fue distribuyendo en las mesas jarros con un sabroso caldo de camarón. Se habían preparado cuatro enormes cazuelas poblanas de arroz con carne de cerdo, nopales en pipián verde, estofado de frutas y pollitos a la piña. En los platones se encontraban pescado blanco de Pátzcuaro, manitas de cerdo, pechugas de pollo en escabeche y ropa vieja. Tampoco podían faltar las grandes ensaladeras, una con nopalitos, cebolla, jitomate y queso desmoronado, y la otra con lechugas romanas revueltas con berros, aguacates partidos, jitomates y cebolla. En platos de barro se dispusieron varias salsas: borracha, mexicana, de tomate con cilantro y de chile cascabel con jitomate asado.

Los postres ocupaban los centros de las mesas. Había, además de dulce de camote con piña, natillas y flan de piñón, cazuelas llenas de los tradicionales dulces mexicanos, de esos que venden todavía en el mercado de La Merced. A Frida le gustaban especialmente los merengues, los muéganos, las trompadas y las charamuscas, pues le recordaban su infancia, cuando, al salir de la escuela, podía jugar un volado con su dulcero favorito y ganar dos o tres de estos apetitosos manjares infantiles. Obvio es decir que los muéganos, en especial, abundaban en la mesa; Frida había decidido darse su propio regalo de cumpleaños comprándolos por montones.

Dulce de camote con piña

(8 personas)

2 kilos de camote amarillo
1 piña mediana pelada
2 tazas de azúcar
150 gramos de piñones

Los camotes se cuecen hasta que estén suaves, se dejan enfriar un poco, se pelan, se pasan por el prensapapas y se miden 3 tazas de

---

Guadalupe Rivera Marín y Marie-Pierre Colle Corcuera, *Las fiestas de Frida y Diego, recuerdos y recetas*, pp. 204–5, 215–16.

puré. La piña se licua, se cuela y se miden 3 tazas. Se mezcla el jugo de piña con el azúcar y se pone sobre la lumbre hasta obtener una miel espesa (104° C o 220° F en el termómetro especial para dulces). Se añade el camote y se deja sobre la lumbre hasta que se vea el fondo de cazo. Se vierte en el platón de servicio y se adorna con los piñones bien lavados y secos.

EJERCICIOS

SKIMMING FOR MEANING

A Determine the purpose of this selection by observing its title and source, then complete the following sentence.

The titles of this selection and the book from which it is taken indicate that this selection is about ______________________.

B Complete the following exercise.

1 *Arroz con carne de cerdo* is one of four dishes served in a *cazuela.* Name the other three.

______________________ ______________________

____

2 Name the dishes served on *platones.*

______________________ ______________________

______________________ ______________________

3 The *ensaladas* are served on ______________ and include one salad made with ______________, ______________, ______________, and ______________, and another salad made with ______________, ______________, ______________, ______________, and ______________.

4 The *salsas* are served on ______________ and include ______________, ______________, ______________, and ______________.

5 The *postres* have been placed ______________ and include ______________, ______________, and ______________, plus *tradicionales dulces mexicanos* presented in ______________.

6 *Los merengues, los muéganos, las trompadas,* and *las charamuscas* are

______________________.

USING CONTEXT TO GUESS MEANING

C Write what has been done to each of the following ingredients, based on the participle in bold type that follows it.

1 *queso* ***desmoronado*** ______________

2 *aguacate* ***partido*** ______________

3 *lechugas* ***revueltas*** ______________

4 *jitomate* ***asado*** ______________

D Write the meaning of each word or phrase that appears in bold type.

1 *apetitosos* ***manjares*** *infantiles* ______________

2 ***estofado*** *de frutas* ______________

3 ***manitas*** *de cerdo* ______________

4 ***pechugas*** *de pollo* ______________

5 *los camotes* ***se cuecen*** *hasta que estén suaves* ______________

6 ***se miden*** *tres tazas* ______________

7 *la piña se licua,* ***se cuela*** ______________

8 *se pone sobre* ***la lumbre*** ______________

9 *hasta obtener una miel* ***espesa*** ______________

E What kind of dish do you think would be called *"ropa vieja"*?

____

F Complete the following sentence.

When Frida was a child, she used to ______________
jugar un volado

with her favorite ______________ in order to get
dulcero

______________________________.
dos o tres de estos apetitosos manjares

FORMING COMPOUND WORDS

G Write the Spanish compound noun and its English meaning in the space provided.

	VERB	NOUN	COMPOUND WORD	ENGLISH MEANING
	abrir	*lata*	abrelatas	can opener
1	*abrir*	*botella*	______________	bottle opener
2	*lavar*	*plato*	______________	______________
3	*tocar*	*disco*	______________	______________

4 What did Frida use to purée the *camote*?

______________ ______________

DESCRIBING A CONTINUING ACTIVITY WITH A VERB + GERUND

Spanish uses certain verbs followed by a gerund to indicate a continuing activity.

ir* + *-ndo

El muchacho ***va recogiendo*** *piedras.*	The boy **goes along picking up** rocks.

andar* + *-ndo

El joven ***anda silbando*** *por la calle.*	The boy **goes** down the street **whistling**.
La chica ***anda diciendo*** *que es mi novia.*	The girl **goes around saying** she's my girlfriend.

seguir* + *-ndo

La mamá ***sigue cocinando****.*	The mother **continues to cook**.
Los chicos ***siguen hablando****.*	The kids **keep on talking**.

H Write the meaning of the phrase that appears in bold type.

"Frida ***fue distribuyendo*** *jarros..."* ______________

Pastel chabela

Ingredientes

175 gramos de azúcar granulada de primera
800 gramos de harina de primera, tamizada tres veces
17 huevos
Raspadura de un limón

Manera de hacerse

En una cacerola se ponen 5 yemas de huevo, 4 huevos enteros y el azúcar. Se baten hasta que la masa espesa y se le anexan 2 huevos enteros más. Se sigue batiendo y cuando vuelve a espesar se le agregan otros 2 huevos completos, repitiendo este paso hasta que se terminan de incorporar todos los huevos, de dos en dos. Para elaborar el pastel de boda de Pedro con Rosaura, Tita y Nacha habían tenido que multiplicar por diez las cantidades de esta receta pues en lugar de un pastel para dieciocho personas tenían que preparar uno para ciento ochenta. ¡El resultado da 170 huevos! Y esto significaba que habían tenido que tomar medidas para tener reunida esta cantidad de huevos, de excelente calidad, en un mismo día.

Para lograrlo fueron poniendo en conserva desde hacía varias semanas los huevos que ponían las gallinas de mejor calidad. Este método se utilizaba en el rancho desde época inmemorial para proveerse durante el invierno de este nutritivo y necesario alimento. El mejor tiempo para esta operación es por los meses de agosto y septiembre. Los huevos que se destinen a la conservación deben ser muy frescos. Nacha prefería que fueran del mismo día. Se ponen los huevos en una vasija que se llena de cebo de carnero derretido, próximo a enfriarse, hasta cubrirlos por completo. Esto basta para garantizar su buen estado por varios meses. Ahora que si se desea conservarlos por más de un año, se colocan los huevos en una orza y se cubren con una lechada de un tanto de cal por diez de agua. Después se tapan muy bien para interceptar el aire y se guardan en la bodega. Tita y Nacha habían elegido la primera opción pues no necesitaban conservar los huevos por tantos meses. Junto a ellas, bajo la mesa de la cocina,

---

Laura Esquivel, *Como agua para chocolate*, pp. 30–32.

tenían la vasija donde los habían puesto y de ahí los tomaban para elaborar el pastel.

El esfuerzo fenomenal que representaba el batir tantos huevos empezó a hacer estragos en la mente de Tita cuando iban apenas por los cien huevos batidos. Le pareció inalcanzable llegar a la cifra de 170.

EJERCICIO

USING YOUR READING SKILLS

- Skim for the general idea.
- Scan for details.
- Recognize cognates.
- Use word endings to identify parts of speech and understand a word's role in a sentence.
- Examine the context of unfamiliar words to guess overall meaning.

A Answer the following questions.

1 *¿Quiénes cocinan?* ______________________________

2 *¿Qué preparan?* ______________________________

¿Para qué lo preparan? ______________________________

3 *¿Para cuántas personas es?* ______________

4 *¿Cuántos huevos necesitan?* ______________

5 *Para conservar los huevos, ¿en qué se ponen?* ______________________________

____

6 *¿Cuáles son los mejores meses para hacer esta operación?*

____

7 *¿Ésta es una receta auténtica o de fantasía?* ______________________________

8 *De las recetas que has leído en esta sección, ¿cuál te apetece más?*

____

La música

Discos

30 canciones en la mochila

Labordeta. Fonomusic

3.675 ptas.

Este doble disco contiene una selección de los temas más conocidos del cantautor aragonés. Un trabajo cargado de compromiso social.

Son del Sur, Vol.2

EMI

2.995 ptas.

Un repertorio perfecto para estar al día en lo que a flamenco se refiere, con artistas como Tomatito, Navajita Plateá, Chano Lobato y Remedios Amaya.

Peces de ciudad

Ana Belén. BMG/Ariola

2.695 ptas.

Un sinfin de sentimientos aderezados con buenas letras y hermosas melodías. Ana Belén vuelve a demostrar que todo lo que hace siempre sabe a éxito.

Buenos Días

EMI

2.595 ptas.

Más que música para despertar, este disco resulta más apropiado para momentos de relajación. Suaves sinfonías para escuchar con los ojos cerrados.

Tsanca. Tierra Virgen

Sergio L.González. Ingo

3.495 ptas.

Después de muchos años dando conciertos y componiendo para otros artistas, el cantautor publica su primer disco. Un viaje a América latina al son de ritmos étnicos.

Exciter

Depeche Mode. Virgin

2.795 ptas.

Tras *The Singles,* un disco que recopilaba sus grandes éxitos, Depeche Mode inicia una nueva etapa creativa con sonidos diferentes y ritmos más variados.

Cambio 16, 18 de junio de 2001, p. 75.

EJERCICIO

SKIMMING FOR MEANING

A Answer the following questions.

1 What are CDs called in Spanish? ______________________________

2 Which of these CDs has a selection of flamenco music?

____

3 Is *"Buenos Días"* good for waking up or winding down?

____

4 Which CD demonstrates a new, creative period for the musicians?

____

5 Which two of these CDs represent singers who write their own songs?

______________________________ ______________________________

6 Which of these is a first CD for the artist? ______________________________

7 Which artist has been continuously successful with good lyrics and beautiful melodies? ______________________________

8 Which of these CDs represents a "best of" selection?

____

La música y vitalidad de Compay Segundo

Con la película y el disco de "Buena Vista Social Club" ha surgido un nuevo interés en la música del son cubano y en su intérprete más destacado, Compay Segundo. Este cantante, compositor e inventor (creó un instrumento nuevo, el armónico, que es híbrido de la guitarra y el tres), se hizo famoso años atrás, primero como la mitad del dúo Los Compadres, luego como miembro del conjunto Matamoros, en el que tocó junto a Benny More.

Pensando que su música ya estaba fuera de moda, cambiada por los ritmos modernos, este gran músico permaneció más de 15 años sin entrar en los estudios de grabación, dejando a sus contemporáneos, que lo veneraron cuando eran jóvenes, conformarse con escucharlo en discos. Pero ahora, a los 94 años, el señor está más animado que nunca, ha anunciado nuevos proyectos artísticos y además, su deseo de tener un sexto hijo. «Si estoy mal de salud, no hay un cubano vivo en la isla. Mi segundo tiempo lo he logrado a los 94 años, y cuando llegue a la edad de mi abuela (115), yo voy a pedir prórroga», afirmó recientemente.

Los musicólogos de este país caribeño insisten en que el son cubano es la base de la moderna salsa. Puede ser. Lo cierto es que Compay Segundo y sus canciones más famosas—"Chan Chan", "La Negra Tomasa" y "Las Flores de la Vida"—ya son reconocidas y queridas en el mundo entero.

EJERCICIOS

SKIMMING FOR MEANING

A Read the selection quickly, then answer the following questions.

1 Whom is this selection about? ____________________

2 Where is he from? ____________________

Adaptada de un artículo de www.EsMas.com.

3 How old is he? ____________

4 What does he do?

____

5 What are his three best-known pieces?

____________ ____________

____

6 What precipitated a resurgence of interest in the Cuban sound?

____

USING COGNATES TO DETERMINE MEANING

B The following Spanish words have English cognates. Write the English equivalent of each one.

Nouns (*Sustantivos*)

1 *la música* ____________
2 *la vitalidad* ____________
3 *el disco* ____________
4 *el interés* ____________
5 *el compositor* ____________
6 *el inventor* ____________
7 *el instrumento* ____________
8 *el híbrido* ____________
9 *la guitarra* ____________
10 *el dúo* ____________
11 *el miembro* ____________
12 *el ritmo* ____________
13 *el músico* ____________
14 *el estudio* ____________
15 *el contemporáneo* ____________
16 *el proyecto* ____________
17 *el tiempo* ____________
18 *el musicólogo* ____________
19 *la base* ____________

Adjectives (*Adjetivos*)

1 *famoso* ____________
2 *moderno* ____________
3 *animado* ____________
4 *segundo* ____________
5 *caribeño* ____________
6 *reconocido* ____________
7 *entero* ____________

Verbs (*Verbos*)

1 *crear* ____________
2 *venerar* ____________
3 *anunciar* ____________
4 *afirmar* ____________
5 *insistir* ____________

USING CONTEXT TO DETERMINE MEANING

C The following words, which do not appear in the selection, have cognates in English. Write the English cognate, then find a word in the selection that most likely has a similar meaning; write this word in the last column.

	SPANISH WORD	ENGLISH COGNATE	WORD IN SELECTION WITH SIMILAR MEANING
1	*filme*	______________	______________
2	*grupo*	______________	______________
3	*extensión*	______________	______________
4	*famoso*	______________	______________
5	*aparecer*	______________	______________
6	*satisfacerse*	______________	______________

D Read the following sentences, then write the meaning of each word or phrase that appears in bold type.

1 *El armónico es híbrido de la guitarra y el* ***tres****.* ______________

2 *Se hizo famoso unos años* ***atrás****.* ______________

3 *Como miembro del conjunto Matamoros,* ***tocó junto a*** *Benny More.*

____

4 *Pensó que su música fue* ***cambiada por*** *ritmos modernos.*

____

5 *El músico* ***permaneció*** *15 años sin hacer un disco.* ______________

6 *Hacen los discos en los estudios de* ***grabación****.* ______________

Los premios Grammy Latinos

¿Es posible definir la música latina como un solo género? Claro que no. Los tipos de música varían muchísimo, tanto que sería imposible clasificarlos de una manera definitiva. Hay géneros de música que son típicos de una región, como el mariachi mexicano y el tango argentino. Hay música folclórica que refleja la tradición de culturas étnicas y música popular que representa lo popular de cada década. Hoy en día está bastante de moda la fusión, es decir, la mezcla de un tipo de música con otros. Cada género merece reconocimiento y es difícil comprender cómo puede competir para un premio un género con otros distintos.

Sin embargo, para el premio anual de los Grammy Latinos, que se realiza cada año en Los Ángeles, California, compiten representantes de diversos tipos de música que no parecen tener nada que ver el uno con el otro. En concreto, entre las nominaciones de este año se encuentran, entre otros muchos, los nombres de Plácido Domingo, el magnífico tenor de ópera; Pepe Aguilar, el actual gigante de la canción ranchera mexicana; el rockero colombiano Juan Esteban Aristizabal, mejor conocido por sus aficionados como "Juanés", la atractiva joven neoyorquina Christina Aguilera, que canta pop-R&B; la romántica brasileña Bebel Gilberto, cantante de voz suave y seductiva; el Sindicato Argentino del Hip Hop; y Luis Miguel, maestro mexicano del bolero. También estará en el espectáculo el famoso cantante melódico de España, Julio Iglesias, pero no como nominación, sino como un tributo a sus logros profesionales y filantrópicos. Al parecer, lo único que tienen en común estos músicos es que hablan español, o por lo menos, sus padres o abuelos lo hablaban.

En todo caso, el espectáculo de los premios Grammy Latinos ofrece una gran oportunidad para conocer a los músicos y los géneros nuevos de la rica y diversa población hispana.

EJERCICIOS

SCANNING FOR INFORMATION

A List the musicians mentioned in this selection, then write the type of music each performs.

	MÚSICO	*GÉNERO DE MÚSICA*
1	______________	______________
2	______________	______________
3	______________	______________
4	______________	______________
5	______________	______________
6	______________	______________
7	______________	______________
8	______________	______________

B How many countries are represented by musicians mentioned in this selection? ______________

USING COGNATES TO DETERMINE MEANING

C Write the English equivalent of the following words.

Sustantivos

1	*gigante*	______________	6	*tributo*	______________
2	*representante*	______________	7	*rockero*	______________
3	*tenor*	______________	8	*nominación*	______________
4	*ópera*	______________	9	*población*	______________
5	*tipo*	______________	10	*oportunidad*	______________

Adjetivos

1	*posible*	______________	5	*romántico*	______________
2	*anual*	______________	6	*filantrópico*	______________
3	*profesional*	______________	7	*rico*	______________
4	*diverso*	______________	8	*seductivo*	______________

Verbos

1	*nominar*	________	5	*definir*	________
2	*opinar*	________	6	*competir*	________
3	*mezclar*	________	7	*incluir*	________
4	*ofrecer*	________			

Beware of "false cognates"—words that look similar but have different meanings in English and Spanish. Following are Spanish words with their true English meaning.

verdadero	actual
realmente	actually
actual	current/present
actualmente	currently
corriente	ordinary
un espectáculo	a show

D Complete the following sentences.

1 *Pepe Aguilar es el* ________ (current) *gigante de la canción ranchera.*

2 *Vamos a ver el* ________ (show) *en la televisión.*

3 *Él es* ________ (actually) *un gran cantante.*

4 *Él no es un cantante* ________ (ordinary).

USING WORD ENDINGS TO DETERMINE MEANING

The suffix *-nte* can indicate a person who performs a certain action.

cantar	to sing	*el cantante*	male singer
		la cantante	female singer

E Using the same pattern as above, complete the following sentences.

1 *Christina Aguilera* ***representa*** *a Nueva York. Ella es* ________ *de Nueva York.*

2 *Carlos* ***preside*** *en todas las reuniones del club. Carlos es* ________ *del club.*

3 *Los brasileños* ***residen*** *en Brasil. Los brasileños son* ________ *de Brasil.*

4 *Las personas que* ***inmigran*** *a un país son* ________.

5 *Mi madre* ***ayuda*** *al médico. Es su mejor* ________.

English nouns that end in *-tion/-sion* often have cognates that end in *-ción/-sión* in Spanish. These nouns are always feminine. In the singular, these nouns have a written accent, which is dropped when they are made plural.

F Write the Spanish equivalent of the following English nouns.

1 the population ______________________

2 the nominations ______________________

3 the position ______________________

4 the attractions ______________________

5 the section ______________________

6 the representation ______________________

7 the organizations ______________________

8 the competition ______________________

USING CONTEXT TO DETERMINE MEANING

G The following three sentences have the same basic meaning.

La música rap es muy ***distinta*** *de la música clásica.*
La música rap y la música clásica ***no tienen nada en común****.*
La música rap ***no tiene nada que ver*** *con la música clásica.*

1 The word *distinto* in isolation looks like "distinct." However, when you read it in the context of the first example above, you can guess that it means

______________________.

2 Write the English equivalent of each sentence above.

____

____

____

3 The word *premio* in isolation looks a lot like "premium." When read in the context *los premios Grammy,* you know that it means ______________________.

4 The word *logros* gives no real clue to its meaning. However, from the context *como un tributo a sus logros profesionales y filantrópicos* you can conclude that it means ______________________.

Los Rabanes

Oriundos de la ciudad de Chitré, Panamá, ubicada en la provincia de Herrera, a aproximadamente tres horas de distancia de la ciudad capital, estos jóvenes talentosos están nominados a Mejor Interpretación Vocal de Grupo en la segunda entrega del Grammy Latino.

La banda la componen Emilio Reguiera, Christian Torres y Javier Saavedra, tres inquietos músicos que, aunque hacen todos sus arreglos ellos mismos, cuando graban, contratan músicos invitados para completar la instrumentación. Han sido autodidactas, es decir, músicos "de oído", dedicados a ir a los escenarios y a resaltar los ritmos que les gustan con una mezcla de ritmos duros de rock y otros ritmos. Identifican a su música como un ritmo animal muy cambiante y sin límites. A la música le ponen lo autóctono panameño como el calipso, y le agregan el reggae, el son haitiano, la salsa y el ritmo cubano.

Los tres músicos, que aún conservan su naturalidad y sencillez, han realizado presentaciones en México, Puerto Rico, Estados Unidos (Chicago, Nueva York, Los Ángeles) y en Europa, logrando el reconocimiento y aceptación del público juvenil que se magnetiza y entra en un estado de histérica alegría con su singular estilo. Cuentan con la ayuda de uno de los productores más reconocidos y exitosos del ambiente musical, Emilio Stefan, y sueñan con conquistar el mercado internacional.

EJERCICIOS

SKIMMING FOR MEANING

A Read the entire selection without the aid of a dictionary, then answer the following questions.

1 Where are *Los Rabanes* from? ____________________________

2 What prize have they been nominated for? ____________________________

Adaptada de Maribel de Villareal, "Desde Panamá Los Rabanes al Grammy Latino", Diarionet.

3 How many are in the group, and what are their names? ____________

____

4 What rhythms do they mix to achieve their unique sound?

____

5 Where have they performed (other than in their native country)?

____

6 What is their manager's name? ________________________

USING FORM AND CONTEXT TO DETERMINE MEANING

B The words below are difficult to define in isolation. However, when we look at their forms and at the words around them, we can make good guesses at their meaning.

1 ***oriundos***
The *-os* ending shows that it is a masculine plural noun or adjective. We can link it to the nearest masculine plural noun found in the sentence, *jóvenes*, and determine that it describes that noun. With this information, plus the context *oriundos de la ciudad de Chitré*, we figure out that

oriundos means ________________________.

2 ***ubicada***
The ending *-ada* tells us that the word is an adjective derived from the participle; since it is feminine singular, it refers to the preceding feminine singular noun, *ciudad de Chitré.* With this information, plus the context *ubicada en la provincia de Herrera,* we decide that *ubicada* means

________________________.

3 ***entrega***
The ending *-a* indicates that this could be a third-person singular verb or a feminine singular noun or adjective. Because it immediately follows an article + adjective, *la segunda*, we determine that it is a noun. From this information and from the words that follow (*del Grammy Latino*), we infer that *entrega*

means ________________________.

4 ***autóctono***
The *-o* ending could indicate a masculine singular noun or adjective. However, its occurrence after *lo* marks it as an adjective used as an abstract noun, modified by *panameño.* With the example of *el calipso* as *lo autóctono*

panameño, we guess that *autóctono* means ________________________.

5 ***logrando***
The ending *-ndo* indicates that this is the gerund form of the verb *lograr*, used to show action in progress. The context *logrando reconocimiento y aceptación* shows that *logrando* probably means

________________________.

Tomatito

«No entiendo el nuevo flamenco»

El nuevo disco de José Fernández Torres, *Tomatito* (Almería, 1958), vuelve a ofrecer flamenco del bueno, con alguna que otra sorpresa, como una *canción turca* acompañada de orquesta, y una rumba en la que toca junto al famoso jazzista George Benson. Y no faltan, por supuesto, las bulerías, las soleás, las tarantas... y es que Tomatito—que acompañó a Camarón durante casi 20 años, que ha recorrido medio mundo, ganado dos Grammy, actuado junto a Elton John o Frank Sinatra y colaborado en películas como *Pacto con el diablo,* entre otras cosas—tiene claras sus raíces y se considera flamenco sobre todas las cosas.

¿Cómo ha sido la experiencia de trabajar con George Benson?

JOSÉ FERNÁNDEZ TORRES Ha sido maravilloso, porque nunca pensé que quisiera grabar conmigo. El hecho de que me abriera su casa y de trabajar con él en los estudios de Nueva York ha sido una experiencia increíble.

¿Tienen algo en común el flamenco y el jazz?

JFT Muchas cosas. No tenemos la misma música, ni los mismos acordes, pero compartimos el sentimiento. Da igual si es un viejo gitano cantando en la fragua o un *blues* antiguo. Nuestra música expresa el sentir del pueblo.

«Paseo de los castaños» es un disco muy variado: tangos, soleás, bulerías... y también jazz y una canción turca. ¿Es usted un artista abierto a otras músicas?

JFT Yo creo que sí. Un solista de guitarra tiene que salir a acompañar, lo cual te obliga a escuchar a otros músicos. Eso se refleja en mi trabajo, aunque sin perder la identidad. Vengo de una familia y una cultura musical flamenca y todo lo que toque sonará siempre a flamenco.

Preguntarle por Camarón es inevitable, ya que trabajaron juntos muchos años. ¿Cuál es el mejor recuerdo que guarda de él?

Cambio 16, 18 de junio de 2001, pp. 74–75.

JFT La humildad que tenía y el hecho de ser un revolucionario del cante y el mejor de nuestra generación. Él me enseñó todo lo que sé.

Ya que habla de Camarón como revolucionario, ¿qué opina de los llamados «nuevos flamencos»?

JFT Para mí, los nuevos flamencos son Camarón y Paco de Lucía. Ellos pusieron el flamenco de moda en su momento, hace más de 20 años. Yo no he escuchado un disco más moderno ni con más ideas que el último de Camarón. Ese «nuevo flamenco» yo, por lo que soy y de donde vengo, la verdad, no lo entiendo.

En su trayectoria profesional también hay incursiones en el cine: «Flamenco», de Saura; «Pacto con el diablo», con Al Pacino... ¿Le gusta participar en bandas sonoras?

JFT Sin duda. Me hace ilusión eso de ponerle música a las imágenes, de darles vida.

¿Cuáles son sus proyectos más inmediatos?

JFT De momento, promocionar este disco. Luego me voy a Europa a hacer el circuito de jazz, después a Japón, a México... siempre salen cosillas sobre la marcha.

EJERCICIOS

SKIMMING FOR THE GENERAL IDEA

A Look at the format of this selection, read the first paragraph, then answer the following questions.

1 What kind of reporting does this selection represent?
- ☐ an interview (*entrevista*)
- ☐ a biographical sketch (*biografía*)
- ☐ a review of a concert (*crítica*)

2 What *género* does Tomatito's music represent? ______________________

3 What are three special sounds of this music?

______________________ ______________________

____

4 What are two other sounds incorporated in his music?

______________________ ______________________

5 Whom did Tomatito once accompany? ______________________

For how long? ______________________

6 What important prizes has he won? ______________________

7 With whom has he performed?

______________________ ______________________

____

8 In what movies can his music be heard?

______________________ ______________________

USING WORD ENDINGS TO DETERMINE MEANING

One way to identify a performer is by the suffix *-ista,* which can refer to a male or a female.

Juan es ***el artista****.*
Isabel es ***la artista****.*

B Write the Spanish equivalent of the following English phrases.

the creative performer (male) el artista

1 the guitar player (female) ______________________
2 the solo performer (male) ______________________
3 the saxophone player (male) ______________________
4 the jazz artist (female) ______________________
5 the cello player (female) ______________________
6 the violin players (female) ______________________
7 the pianists (male and female) ______________________

USING CONTEXT TO DETERMINE MEANING

C Write the English meaning of the phrases that appear in bold type.

1 *Él es mi amigo. Lo sé* ***por el hecho de que*** *me ayuda.*

____

2 *¿Quieres chocolate o vainilla? —**Da igual.** Me gustan los dos.*

____

3 *La salsa está* ***de moda*** *hoy en día. La bailan en todas partes.*

____

4 *La música de Tomatito aparece en dos películas. Le gusta trabajar en* ***bandas sonoras****.* ______________________

5 *Me encanta la música de Tomatito. Voy a su próximo concierto y,* ***por supuesto****, tengo muchos discos suyos.* ______________________

El tango

Los argentinos dicen que el tango es un sentimiento triste que se baila. Este baile y la música que lo acompaña nacieron en los puertos de Buenos Aires a principios del siglo XX. El baile se consideraba vulgar y fue condenado como vehículo de inmoralidad por el Papa Pío X, hasta que él mismo vio una exhibición de la danza y levantó la prohibición. Fue popular en París, luego en Nueva York y en Tokio, y hoy en día hay academias de tango en Alemania, Brasil, Bélgica, Cuba, Holanda, México y Chile, y además, los países Japón, Israel, Inglaterra y Portugal tienen academias en formación. La Academia Nacional del Tango está, por supuesto, en Buenos Aires. Además de esto, se organizan tours a esta ciudad donde lo único que hacen los participantes es practicar tango desde la mañana hasta la próxima madrugada, todos los días. Pero si uno quiere bailar tango, no tiene que ir a una academia, sólo tiene que dirigirse a cualquier ciudad grande del mundo y buscar el "tango hotline" en la guía telefónica para encontrarse con un grupo de "tangueros" que le darán la bienvenida a su próxima "milonga".

EJERCICIO

SKIMMING FOR GENERAL MEANING

A Read the selection quickly, then answer the following questions.

1 Where did the tango originate? ______________________

2 Was it considered an acceptable dance for the general public? __________

3 Who banned it, and why did he reverse his decision?

____

4 In what cities was it popular early on? ______________________

5 Where is the National Academy of the Tango? ______________________

6 Are there academies in other countries? __________

7 Where can one go for "round the clock" tango lessons?

____

8 Where else can one go to get started with tango?

____

9 What are tango dancers called? ______________________

10 What are tango parties called? ______________________

ARGENTINA

Si se calla el cantor

Una canción folclórica por Horacio Guarany

Si se calla el cantor,
calla la vida.
Porque la vida
misma es toda un canto.

Si se calla el cantor,
muere de espanto.
La esperanza, la luz y la alegría.

Si se calla el cantor,
se quedan solos los humildes gorriones, de los diarios.
Los obreros del puerto,
se persignan.
Quién habrá de luchar por sus salarios.

Qué ha de ser de la vida,
si el que canta, no levanta su voz en las tribunas.
Por el que sufre,
por el que no hay ninguna razón que lo condene a andar sin manta.

Si se calla el cantor,
muere la rosa.
De qué sirve la rosa,
sin el canto.
Debe el canto ser luz,
sobre los campos,
iluminando siempre, a los de abajo.

Que no calle el cantor,
porque el silencio cobarde apaña la maldad, que oprime.
No saben los cantores de agachadas:
no callarán jamás de frente al crimen.

Que se levanten todas las banderas
cuando el cantor se plante con su grito.
Que mil guitarras desangren en la noche,
una inmortal canción al infinito.

Si se calla el cantor, calla la vida.

EJERCICIOS

USING WORD FORMS TO DETERMINE MEANING

Spanish verbs that require the reflexive pronoun *se* often do not have reflexive meaning in English. The selection has the following verbs of this type.

se calla el cantor	the singer is silent
se quedan solos los gorriones	the sparrows are all alone
se persignan los obreros	the workers make the sign of the cross
se planta el cantor	the singer stops/gives up

SKIMMING FOR MEANING

A What is the general message of this song?

____

SCANNING FOR DETAILS

B Answer the following questions.

1 According to the selection, what is "life itself"? ____________________

2 If the singer is silent, what will die? ____________________

3 What should a song do in the countryside?

____

4 What is cowardly and covers up evil? ____________________

5 What will end if the singer is silent? ____________________

Recuerdos de la niñez

PUERTO RICO

Cantando en la escuela

Arr yu slepin? Arr yu slepin?
Bro der Yon, Bro der Yon.
Mornin belsar rin gin
Mornin belsar rin gin
Din din don. Din din don.

A Miss Jiménez le gustaba enseñarnos el inglés por medio de las canciones, y aprendimos todas las canciones fonéticamente, con poca idea de lo que querían decir en español. Trató de enseñarnos "America the Beautiful", pero tuvo que desistir cuando nos enredamos en "fó espechos scays" (*for spacious skies*) y "ambur ueys ofgrén" (*amber waves of grain*).

A la misma vez nos enseñó "La borinqueña", la cual decía que Borinquén era la hija del mar y el sol. A mí me gustaba pensar en nuestra islita como una mujer cuyo cuerpo era un jardín de flores, sus pies acariciados por las olas del mar, sus cielos sin nubes. Me gustaba especialmente la parte de cuando a sus playas llegó Colón y exclamó, lleno de admiración: "¡Ay! Esta es la linda tierra que busco yo".

Pero mi canción patriótica favorita era "En mi viejo San Juan", en la cual el poeta le dice adiós al viejo San Juan y llama a Puerto Rico "diosa del mar, reina de palmar".

EJERCICIO

USING YOUR READING SKILLS

- Skim for the general idea.
- Scan for details.
- Recognize cognates.
- Use word endings to identify parts of speech and understand a word's role in a sentence.
- Examine the context of unfamiliar words to guess their meaning.

Esmeralda Santiago, *Cuando era puertorriqueña*, pp. 83–84.

A Answer the following questions.

1 *¿Cómo aprenden los niños el inglés?* ______________________________

2 *¿Cómo se llama la maestra?* ______________________

3 *¿Entienden los niños la letra de las canciones?* ____________

4 *¿Qué canción les dio problemas de pronunciación?*

____

5 *¿A qué isla se refiere "La Borinqueña"?* ________________________

6 *¿Con qué se compara la isla en esta canción?* ____________________

7 *¿Quién dijo que ésa era la linda tierra que buscaba?*

____

8 *¿Cuál era la canción favorita de la niña?* ______________________

ESPAÑA

El coro de la escuela

...Y la asquerosa Guindilla también estaba allí, con una varita en la mano, erigida, espontáneamente, en directora.

Al entrar ellos, les ordenó a todos por estatura; después levantó la varita por encima de la cabeza y dijo:

—Veamos. Quiero ensayar con vosotros el «Pastora Divina» para cantarlo el día de la Virgen. Veamos —repitió.

Hizo una señal a Trino y luego bajó la varita y los niños y niñas cantaron cada uno por su lado:

Pas-to-ra Di-vi-naaa
Seee-guir-te yo quie-rooo...

Cuando ya empezaban a sintonizar las cuarenta y dos voces, la Guindilla mayor puso un cómico gesto de desolación y dijo:

—¡Basta, basta! No es eso. No es «Pas», es «Paaas». Así:

«Paaas-to-ra Di-vi-na; Seee-guir-te yo quie-rooo; poor va-lles y o-te-roos; Tuuus hue-llas en pooos». Veamos —repitió.

Dio con la varita en la cubierta del armonio y de nuevo atrajo la atención de todos. Los muros del templo se estremecieron bajo los agudos acentos infantiles. Al poco rato, la Guindilla puso un acusado gesto de asco. Luego señaló al Moñigo con la varita.

Miguel Delibes, *El camino*, pp. 171–73.

—Tú puedes marcharte, Roque; no te necesito. ¿Cuándo cambiaste la voz?

Roque, el Moñigo, humilló la mirada:

—¡Qué sé yo! Dice mi padre que ya de recién nacido berreaba con voz de hombre.

Aunque cabizbajo, el Moñigo decía aquello con orgullo, persuadido de que un hombre bien hombre debe definirse desde el nacimiento. Los primeros de la escuela acusaron su manifestación con unas risitas de superioridad. En cambio, las niñas miraron al Moñigo con encendida admiración.

EJERCICIO

B Using your reading skills, answer the following questions.

1 *¿Cómo llamaban los niños a la directora?* ____________________

2 *¿Era muy estricta la directora?* ____________________

3 *¿Cuándo iban a cantar el "Pastora Divina"?* ____________________

4 *¿Cuántos niños cantaban al principio?* __________

5 *¿Cómo atraía la directora la atención de los niños?*

____

6 *¿Por qué expulsó a Roque (el Moñigo)?* ____________________

7 *¿Cómo miraron las niñas al Moñigo?* ____________________

PERÚ

Un recital de piano

Para el recital de fin de año, en preparatoria, Julius tenía *My Bony* estudiadísimo, a Susan ni se le pasaba por la mente que podría equivocarse. No miró a su alrededor para que supieran que era su hijo el que estaba tocando, pero sí escuchó con ternura mientras el pobre batallaba con unos inesperados nervios, en realidad tocó un *My Bony* bastante cambiado. ¡Qué importa!, todo el mundo estuvo de acuerdo en que lo hizo con mucho sentimiento.

Así eran los recitales. Tocaban los mejores alumnos, la monjita de las pecas los seleccionaba y los preparaba hasta el último minuto. Ter-

Alfredo Bryce Echenique, *Un mundo para Julius*, pp. 104–5.

minada la repartición de premios salían al escenario y se equivocaban varias veces. Sus mamás se morían de nervios, se preparaban para aplaudir, para morirse cuando uno se quedara a la mitad de la pieza, para aplaudirlos fuertemente como si ya hubieran terminado y salvarlos: no importaba, al final siempre habían tocado con mucho sentimiento. Hasta Rafaelito Lastarria logró tocar en un recital, claro que con trampa porque tenía otra profesora en casa, pero logró terminar su Danza Apache y Susana se sintió tan felicitada. También Juan Lastarria se emocionó e hizo una donación especial para el colegio nuevo.

EJERCICIO

C Using your reading skills, answer the following questions.

1 *¿Cuándo fue el recital?* ____________________

2 *¿Quién tocó "My Bony"?* ____________________

3 *¿Cómo se llamaba la mamá del muchacho?* ____________________

4 *¿Cómo tocó la canción?* ____________________

5 *¿Quiénes tocaban en los recitales?* ____________________

6 *¿Quién los seleccionaba y preparaba?* ____________________

7 *¿De qué se morían las madres?* ____________________

8 *¿Al final, cómo tocaban todos?* ____________________

9 *¿Qué tocó Rafaelito Lastarria?* ____________________

10 *¿Qué hizo su papá después?* ____________________

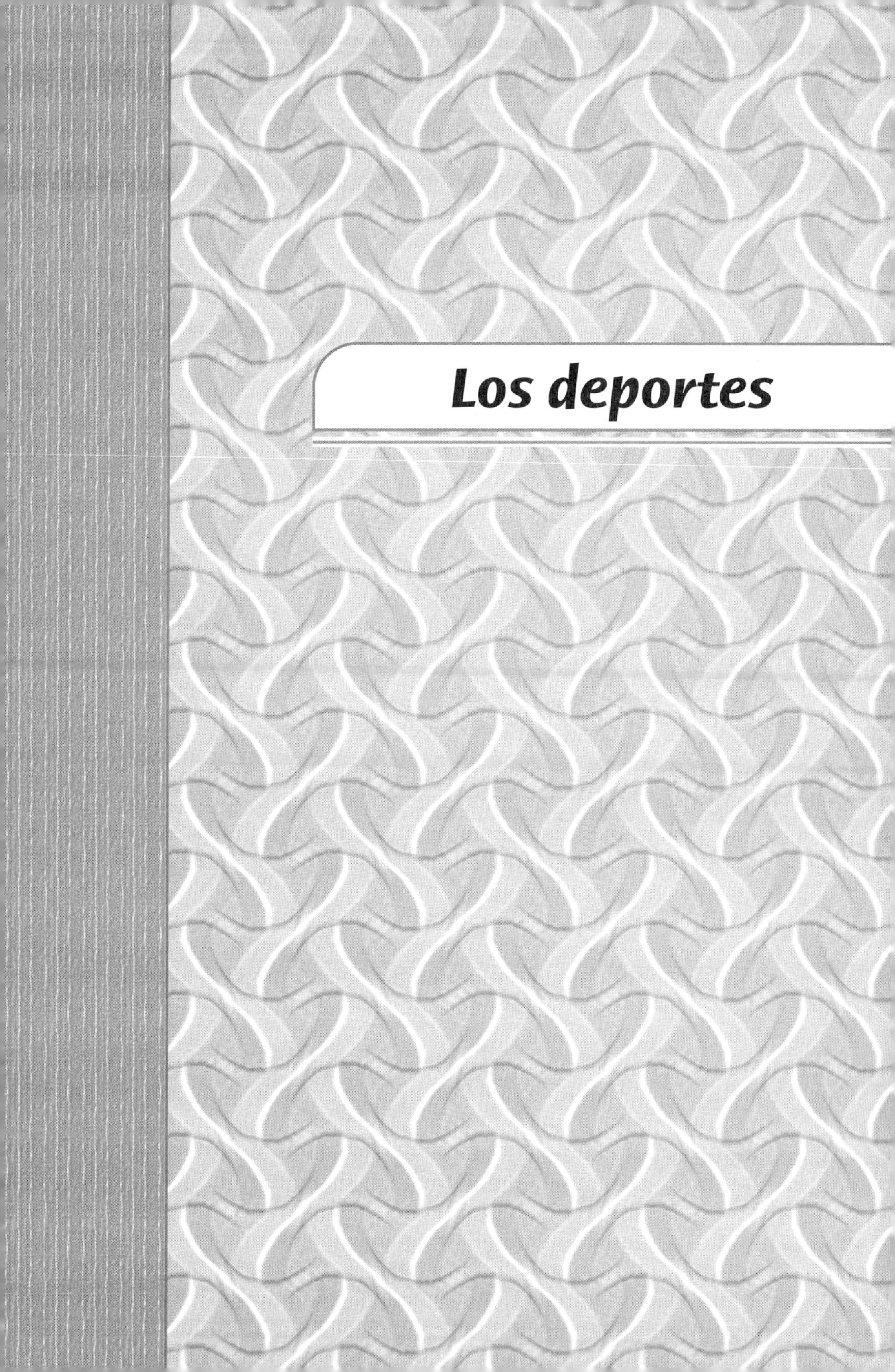

Los deportes

Todos somos Guerreros

En nuestra comunidad de San José la tradición más joven es EL BÉISBOL

JULIO Y AGOSTO		PROMOCIONES
Martes 17 y 31 San José Vs. Pasadena	ESTUDIANTES 2 × 1	Con un boleto entran 2 estudiantes presentando su credencial en la entrada
Miércoles 18 y agosto 01 San José Vs. Pasadena	3 × 3	Con un boleto especial de $75.00 entran: 3 personas y además llévate GRATIS 3 tortas y 3 refrescos
Jueves 19 y agosto 02 San José Vs. Pasadena	CHICA GUERRERA	Las damas que asistan con los colores Guerreros (blanco, negro y rojo) entrada GRATIS acompañadas de un caballero que adquiera su boleto
Viernes 20 y agosto 03 San José Vs. San Miguel	NIÑOS GRATIS	Niños menores de 12 años GRATIS acompañados de un adulto que adquiera su boleto
	LA VICTORIA ASEGURADA	Si los Guerreros ganan hoy, el sábado 2 × 1 en todas las localidades
Domingo 22 San José Vs. San Miguel	DOMINGO FAMILIAR	Con el boleto de Papá entran: Mamá y 2 niños menores de 12 años
"TATO"	La Mascota	Diviértete, participa y gana todos los días con los concursos de la mascota de los Guerreros

ESTADIO CENTRAL

Palcos	$50.00
General	$30.00
Jardines	$10.00

EJERCICIO

SCANNING FOR INFORMATION

A Answer the following questions.

1 What is this flyer announcing, and for what time period?

____

2 When is "ladies' night," and what are the conditions for free entrance?

____

____

3 What are the Guerreros' colors? ______________________________

4 How much is a seat in the balcony? ______________

5 What is the team mascot's name? What happens in his name at every game?

____

6 What can three adults get on the first of August?

____

7 What happens if the Guerreros win on July 20?

____

8 On which dates can children get in free? Can they just walk in without tickets?

____

____

9 What does *domingo familiar* mean? ______________________________

10 What teams are playing on July 31? ______________________________

11 What is the name of the stadium? ______________________________

Noticias de béisbol

1. Los Cachorros de Chicago vs los Cerveceros de Milwaukee

Sammy Sosa conectó tres jonrones e impulsó seis carreras, ayudando a Kevin Tapani a ganar por primera vez en casi once semanas, en la victoria de los Cachorros de Chicago sobre los Cerveceros de Milwaukee por paliza de 16-3. Sosa bateó un jonrón solitario, otro para dos carreras y uno más para tres.

2. Los dominicanos brillaron en las Grandes Ligas

El tercera base Felipe López congeló a los campeones del mundo al pegarles dos tablazos de vuelta entera, y su compatriota Bartolo Colón brilló en el centro del diamante para darle a su equipo un triunfo y confirmar la presencia de la bola dominicana en las Grandes Ligas.

3. Los Azulejos de Toronto vs los Yanquis de Nueva York

En Toronto, el dominicano Felipe López pegó dos vuelacercas y el guardabosques puertorriqueño José Cruz, uno, y los Azulejos de Toronto vencieron 14-0 a los campeones del mundo los Yanquis de Nueva York. López se voló la barda en el cuarto episodio, con uno en los senderos, mientras que en la octava entrada, lo hizo sin gente en el camino, además de que se fue de 5-3 con tres anotadas y cinco remolcadas, para dejar en .242 su promedio de bateo. Cruz pegó de cuatro esquinas en el primer episodio, sin gente en los senderos, para coronar racimo de cinco anotaciones, que pusieron en el camino del triunfo a los Azulejos.

4. Los Indios de Cleveland vs los Medias Rojas de Boston

En Boston, el abridor dominicano Bartolo Colón trabajó más de cinco episodios para guiar el triunfo de los Indios de Cleveland con pizarra de 8-5 ante los Medias Rojas de Boston. Colón (12-10) lanzó cinco episodios y dos tercios, y a pesar de ser castigado con 10 imparables y cuatro anotaciones, dar tres pasaportes y sacar a tres por la vía del

---

Adaptada de un artículo de www.terra.com.

ponche, se adjudicó la victoria. En el ataque lo apoyaron el parador en corto venezolano Omar Vizquel, que se fue de 3-1 con una anotada; el segunda base puertorriqueño Roberto Alomar, ligó de 4-1 con una anotada, mientras que el receptor panameño Einar Díaz conectó de 4-2 con dos anotadas.

5. Los Medias Blancas de Chicago vs los Tigres de Detroit

En Chicago, los Medias Blancas derrotaron 10-1 a los Tigres de Detroit en feria de batazos, en el primer partido de la doble jornada en que el tercera base puertorriqueño José Valentín pegó vuelacercas. Valentín conectó su vigésimo quinto cuadrangular de la temporada con el que abrió la cuenta de su equipo. En el segundo partido, el guardabosques venezolano Magglio Ordóñez volvió a ganar con pizarra de 4-0. Ordóñez pegó cuadrangular con uno en los senderos.

6. Los Vigilantes de Texas vs los Mellizos de Minnesota

En Arlington, los Vigilantes de Texas vencieron 6-5 a los Mellizos de Minnesota, pero siguen en el fondo de la división, mientras que por los derrotados el bateador designado dominicano David Ortiz pegó de 4-1 con anotada y remolcada, y su compatriota el parador en corto Cristian Guzmán ligó de 4-2 con dos anotadas.

7. Los Astros de Houston vs los Rojos de Cincinnati

En Cincinnati, el antesalista mexicano Vinny Castilla lideró el ataque para que los Astros de Houston derrotaran 7-1 a los Rojos de Cincinnati. Castilla, que pegó de 4-3, guió el ataque y en la primera entrada abrió la cuenta de su equipo al aprovechar error de Dmitri Young, para hacer sonar la registradora. El tercera base mexicano anotó tres carreras.

8. Los Cardenales de San Luis vs los Padres de San Diego

En San Diego, los Cardenales de San Luis vencieron 6-1 a los Padres de San Diego, con el apoyo del dominicano Albert Pujols. Pujols llegó a su jonrón 33 de la temporada en la séptima entrada, con uno en los senderos, y en la ofensiva también estuvieron el segunda base Fernando Viña, que pegó de 3-1 con una anotada, y el parador en corto colombiano Edgar Rentería, que ligó de 4-2 con una anotada.

EJERCICIOS

USING COGNATES TO DETERMINE MEANING

A Write the English meaning of the following words and phrases.

1 *el promedio de bateo* ______________________________

2 *un triunfo* ______________________________

3 *su compatriota* ______________________________

4 *el jonrón* ______________________________

5 *el bateador designado* ______________________________

6 *un error* ______________________________

7 *el episodio (hay nueve en un partido de béisbol)* ______________________________

B Read the following sentences, then fill in the blanks.

1 *En un diamante de béisbol, hay tres bases: la primera base,*

______________________________ *y* ______________________________.

2 *Los jugadores que se posicionan en las bases son: el primera base,*

______________________________ *y* ______________________________.

USING ASSOCIATION TO DETERMINE MEANING

C Write in the Spanish name of each team mentioned in the selection.

1 the Cubs ______________________________

2 the Blue Jays ______________________________

3 the Reds ______________________________

4 the Red Sox ______________________________

5 the Tigers ______________________________

6 the Astros ______________________________

7 the Cardinals ______________________________

8 the Yankees ______________________________

9 the Padres ______________________________

10 the White Sox ______________________________

11 the Indians ______________________________

12 the Rangers ______________________________

USING WORD FORMATION TO DETERMINE MEANING

In Spanish, compound nouns are often formed from a verb and a plural noun.

lavar	+ *platos*	→ *el lavaplatos*
to wash	dishes	dishwasher
tocar	+ *discos*	→ *el tocadiscos*
to play	records	record player

D Answer the following questions.

1 If *volar* means "to fly" and *cerca* means "fence," what is a *vuelacercas?*

____

2 If *guardar* means "to watch" and *bosque* means "forest," what is a *guardabosques*? ____________________

3 What do these terms mean in the context of baseball?

____________________ ____________________

E Find the Spanish equivalent of the following English words in the selection and write them below.

1	________ the bat	________ to bat	________ the batter
2	el lanzamiento the pitch	________ to pitch	el lanzador the pitcher
3	________ the run	________ to run	el corredor the runner

The suffix *-azo* can increase the strength of a noun.

un trabajo	a job
un trabajazo	a huge job

F Find two words in the selection that mean "a huge hit with the bat" and write them below.

____________________ ____________________

USING CONTEXT TO DETERMINE MEANING

G Find each of the following Spanish words or phrases in the selection, consider its context, then match it with its best English equivalent in the second column.

1	_____ *la entrada/el episodio*	a	the leadoff batter
2	_____ *el abridor*	b	score
3	_____ *un tercio*	c	doubleheader
4	_____ *el parador en corto*	d	runs
5	_____ *el receptor*	e	a walk
6	_____ *pizarra*	f	shortstop
7	_____ *la doble jornada*	g	inning
8	_____ *carreras/anotadas*	h	catcher
9	_____ *el antesalista*	i	with one out
10	_____ *el pasaporte/el boleto*	j	the strikeout
11	_____ *el ponche*	k	starting pitcher
12	_____ *congelar*	l	to hit
13	_____ *impulsar*	m	to score first
14	_____ *pegar*	n	to take advantage of
15	_____ *abrir la cuenta*	o	to freeze
16	_____ *aprovechar*	p	to bat in
17	_____ *por paliza*	q	whipped
18	_____ *en el sendero*	r	at the bottom
19	_____ *en el fondo*	s	on base
20	_____ *cuadrangular/de cuatro esquinas*	t	with no men on base
21	_____ *remolcadas*	u	a hit
22	_____ *solitario*	v	a home run
23	_____ *imparable*	w	RBIs (runs batted in)

Edgar Martínez

Hoy en día, Edgar Martínez es uno de los mejores bateadores del béisbol. Pregúntele a cualquier fanático de los Yanquis sobre este toletero de Seattle que acabó la serie divisional de 1995 con un doble en la 11ma entrada del quinto juego, aquella que impulsó a Ken Griffey Jr. desde la primera con la carrera ganadora. Ése fue el último juego que Buck Showalter manejó con el uniforme a rayas, mientras que a su vez daba comienzo la era de Joe Torre. Pero, aún después de cinco años, Martínez todavía tiene el bateo prolijo que le otorgara el puesto más alto de la Liga Americana en impulsadas (145) y entre los 10 mejores del año 2000 en promedio (.324).

Martínez siempre ha sido un bateador consistente, alrededor de un promedio de .300, y este año no fue la excepción. Bateó para .314, con un promedio vitalicio de .320. La liga trata de evitar la confrontación directa con su bate, como lo atestiguan sus 973 boletos en toda su carrera. Y parece que no le han dado suficientes boletos, porque se las ha arreglado para acumular un total vitalicio de 235 cuadrangulares hasta el final de la temporada del 2000. Edgar es casi una demoledora humana y lidera a los Marineros en hits (180), promedio de bateo (.324) e impulsadas (145).

Detengámonos a ver un poco el promedio de las tres últimas temporadas de Edgar, las cuales han sido realmente sobresalientes. Ha tenido un promedio de .328 en 538 turnos al bate, ha anotado 91 carreras, 176 hits, 37 dobles, 30 cuadrangulares, 111 impulsadas y 100 bases por bolas. Edgar es un tipo tranquilo, que juega duro y siempre hace el trabajo con plena satisfacción.

EJERCICIOS

USING COGNATES

A Write the Spanish equivalent of the following English words and phrases.

Nouns

1 hit (unstoppable) ____________________

2 batter ____________________

3 baseball ____________________

4 fan ____________________

5 division series ____________________

6 a double ____________________

7 first base ____________________

8 the bat ____________________

9 runs batted in (impelled) ____________________

10 walks (bases on balls) ____________________

Verbs

1 to bat in (impel) ____________________

2 to manage ____________________

3 to bat ____________________

4 to lead ____________________

USING CONTEXT TO DETERMINE MEANING

B Write the English meaning of the words that appear in bold type.

1 *Edgar Martínez es un* ***toletero*** *fuerte, uno de los mejores bateadores del béisbol.* ____________________

2 *Martínez hizo la carrera* ***ganadora*** *en la séptima entrada del partido.*

____

3 *Martínez tiene un promedio* ***vitalicio*** *de .320.* ____________________

4 *Acumuló un total vitalicio de 235 cuadrangulares hasta el final de la* ***temporada*** *del 2000.* ____________________

5 *Edgar es casi una* ***demoledora*** *humana.* ____________________

Javier Quirós vuelve a la pista

Dicen que en ocasiones es necesario hacer un alto en el camino. Para Javier Quirós ese fue de cuatro años y ya le puso fin. La familia "jaló" mucho en aquel momento, mas, como él mismo dice, "todo se acomodó".

El experimentado corredor se encuentra en Estados Unidos, donde participará con la escudería AASCO en las "24 horas de Daytona", que se iniciará el sábado, a las 12 m., y finalizará al día siguiente, a la misma hora. De acuerdo con Jaime Peña, vocero de Quirós, éste se encuentra desde principios de enero entrenándose para la competencia.

Una llamada

"A él lo llamaron a probar los carros de la escudería y de una vez le hicieron la oferta para que se quedara", explicó Peña. Quirós hizo un tiempo por vuelta de 1 minuto, 55 segundos y 8 centésimas; mucho mejor que el récord de 1:57:02. El piloto competirá en la categoría GTS-3, la misma en que compitió y ganó en febrero de 1997, con BMW. También compitió en 1996 con esa misma escudería y obtuvo el tercer lugar. Ese nivel comprende aquellos autos que no sobrepasen los 500 caballos de fuerza. Para esta oportunidad, Quirós será el piloto de un BMW-3, de ocho cilindros y 480 caballos de fuerza. Según explicó el vocero Peña, tendrá dos compañeros en la competencia: Andy Durduck y Craig Stanton. Cada piloto tomará el comando del automóvil por espacio de tres horas y se rotarán.

Para Quirós —según unas declaraciones dadas por intermedio de su vocero—, el prolongado receso no lo afectó en su condición física. "En realidad me mantuve bien, porque corro todas las mañanas y voy al gimnasio", sostuvo el piloto. "Y al segundo día que estuve en Daytona ya estaba como si nada", manifestó. En estos días Javier Quirós agregó a su rutina de acondicionamiento físico las pesas y ejercicios para el cuello y piernas.

---

www.terra.co.cr, 31 de enero de 2002.

Muy difícil

Las 24 horas de Daytona es una de las carreras de resistencia más reconocidas del mundo y cumplirá 40 años con la edición 2002. En declaraciones dadas a la página oficial en Internet de la competencia, Hurley Haywood, quien la ganó en cinco oportunidades, la calificó como "mucho más dura que Le Mans". "Uno tiene 12 horas de oscuridad en Daytona, contra sólo cuatro en Le Mans". "Ganar esta carrera requiere de un gran acoplamiento entre los conductores y los mecánicos. Es como armar un rompecabezas", apuntó Haywood. Este piloto habla con conocimiento de causa pues ganó Le Mans en tres ocasiones. La famosa pista, ubicada en el estado de Florida, fue construida en 1959 por Bill Frances.

EJERCICIOS

SKIMMING FOR MEANING

A Read the entire selection quickly to get a general idea of its meaning, then answer the following questions.

1 Where is Javier Quirós from? ______________________

2 What is his sport? ______________________

3 What competition is he preparing for? ______________________

USING CONTEXT TO DETERMINE MEANING

B The following words may be unfamiliar.

jaló (jalar)	*sobrepasen (sobrepasar)*	*acoplamiento*
escudería	*se rotarán (rotarse)*	
vocero	*agregó (agregar)*	

Read them in the contexts below, then write their meaning in the space provided.

1 *Cuando Javier decidió volver a correr en las competencias, su familia **jaló** mucho.* ______________________

2 *Javier participará con la **escudería** AASCO en Daytona.*

____

3 *Jaime Peña, **vocero** de Quirós, dice que éste está en forma.*

____

4 *Estos autos no **sobrepasan** los 500 caballos de fuerza.*

____

5 *Cada uno de los tres pilotos conducirá tres horas y* ***se rotarán****.*

____

6 *Quirós corre todos los días. Recientemente* ***agregó*** *a su rutina las pesas y otros ejercicios.* ______________________________

7 *Ganar esta carrera requiere de un gran* ***acoplamiento*** *entre los conductores y los mecánicos.* ______________________________

UNDERSTANDING DISCOURSE MARKERS

The word *mas* without an accent mark means "but" or "however."

The word *pues* in certain contexts means "because" or "since."

C Find *mas* and *pues* in the selection, write the sentences in which they appear, and then write an English equivalent for each sentence.

____

____

____

____

____

____

UNDERSTANDING WORD FORMATION

Many compound words in Spanish are formed from a verb and a plural noun.

limpiar	+ *botas*	→ *un limpiabotas*
to clean	boots	"boot cleaner"/shoeshine boy

D Answer the following questions.

1 What verb and noun are combined to form the word *rompecabezas*?

______________________________ ______________________________

2 What does *rompecabezas* mean? ______________________________

REREADING FOR DETAILS

E Read the selection again, then answer the following questions.

1 How long was Javier Quirós's break from racing? ______________________

2 What is the name of his team? ______________________

3 What are the names of the other members?

______________________ ______________________

4 What kind of car will he be driving? ______________________

5 Who is his spokesman? ______________________

6 How did he stay in shape during his break?

____

7 Is he ready for this race? ____________

8 By what authority does Hurley Haywood say that Daytona is much harder than Le Mans?

____

Una hispana en la WNBA

La única hispana en la liga WNBA proviene de Colombia, y fue un encuentro fortuito el que llevó a Levys Torres a un destino en el básquet profesional en Estados Unidos.

Desde su infancia en Colombia, Levys se inclinó por cosas diferentes, pero nunca pensó que una conversación casual con un entrenador de básquetbol le cambiaría la vida. A los 15 años de edad, una Levys adolescente pero ya con estatura poco común, deambulaba por una calle de Barranquilla, cuando Roberto Osorio, un entrenador de su ciudad, la abordó y la invitó a formar parte del equipo que entrenaba.

Torres accedió y comenzó asistiendo dos veces por semana a aprender este deporte. Fue integrante del equipo nacional de Colombia que en 1997 ganó el Torneo Sudamericano. En 1999 la colombiana de 1.93 metros ingresó a la Universidad de Florida State, donde promedió 10.8 puntos y 10 rebotes por partido en su último año.

Torres se convirtió en la primera hispana en ser elegida por la liga, al ser seleccionada en la tercera ronda del draft el 25 de abril de 2001.

Aunque Torres tiene contrato de sólo un año, espera continuar jugando para el Miami Sol, pues le encantan la ciudad y Miami Beach, donde reside. Afirma sentirse como en su propia casa, debido a la influencia latina que existe en esa ciudad que es puente a Latinoamérica.

EJERCICIOS

SKIMMING FOR GENERAL MEANING

A Read the selection quickly, then answer the following questions.

1 Whom is this selection about? ______________________________

2 Where is she from? ______________________________

3 What sport does she play? ______________________________

Adaptada de *Acción Deportiva*, 14 de agosto de 2001, p. 42.

4 What team does she play for? ______________________

5 How many Hispanic women are in this league? ______________________

USING WORD FORMATION TO DETERMINE MEANING

In Spanish, the events of a narrative are expressed in the preterite tense. Most verbs in this tense have the ending *-ó* or *-ió* to relate activities performed by another person (third-person singular).

hablar	to talk	*habló*	he talked/she talked
comer	to eat	*comió*	he ate/she ate
escribir	to write	*escribió*	he wrote/she wrote

B Find the verbs in the selection that describe Levys's activities and write them in the first column. Write the infinitive form of each verb in the second column.

	PRETERITE FORM	INFINITIVE
	llevó	llevar
1	______________________	______________________
2	______________________	______________________
3	______________________	______________________
4	______________________	______________________
5	______________________	______________________
6	______________________	______________________
7	______________________	______________________
8	______________________	______________________
9	______________________	______________________
10	______________________	______________________

C Using your cognate and context skills, write the English meaning of the infinitives in Exercise B.

1	______________________	6	______________________
2	______________________	7	______________________
3	______________________	8	______________________
4	______________________	9	______________________
5	______________________	10	______________________

To describe activities that were already in progress when something else happened, the imperfect tense is used. In this tense, third-person singular verbs end in *-aba* or *-ía.*

hablaba	he was talking/she was talking
comía	he was eating/she was eating
escribía	he was writing/she was writing

D There are two verbs in the imperfect tense in the selection; use them to answer the following questions.

1 What was Levys doing when Roberto Osorio approached her?

____

2 What was Osorio doing during that period?

____

SCANNING FOR DETAILS

E Answer the following questions.

1 How old was Levys when she was recruited? ____________

2 Where was she? ______________________

3 How tall is she? ______________

4 What did her team win in Colombia, and when?

____

5 What university did she attend in the United States, and when?

____

6 How many points and rebounds did she average in her last season?

____

7 When was she drafted into the league? ______________________

8 What was the length of her contract? ______________________

Nicolás Lapentti

Entrevista con Nicolás Lapentti, por Edward Crespo G., para WebWorks

Nicolás nos llamó a WebWorks para disculparse porque llegaría atrasado a su entrevista. Para alguien famoso, ese tipo de gentilezas no son muy comunes, gesto que reforzó aún más nuestra percepción de la sencillez que caracteriza la personalidad de Nicolás Lapentti, un carismático chico de 24 años, que además tiene un forehand mortal y está ranqueado entre los ocho mejores jugadores de tenis del mundo.

Cuando Nicolás llegó a nuestra oficina, iluminó la sala con su sonrisa. Estaba vestido de manera casual, en short y camiseta y por supuesto su infaltable gorra. Estábamos ansiosos de mostrarle los últimos avances de su web page.

Entonces nos pusimos a trabajar.

WEBWORKS *Nicolás, gracias por la entrevista.*

NICOLÁS LAPENTTI Es un gusto para mí.

WW *¿Cuál ha sido el partido que más recuerdas en este año?*

NL Fue en los cuartos de final del Abierto de Australia con Karol Kucera. El partido se prolongó hasta tarde en la noche, estaba extenuado, y el estadio estaba lleno con más de 15.000 hinchas apoyándonos a los dos hasta el final.

WW *¿Cuál fue el resultado del mismo?*

NL Felizmente gané 8-6 en el quinto set; fue muy emocionante.

WW *¿Cuál es el partido que más recuerdas de la Copa Davis?*

NL Fue contra Holanda, yo perdí los dos primeros sets en el cuarto partido contra Holanda. Sentí gran apoyo del público mientras jugaba. No los quería decepcionar. Sabía que tenía que luchar con toda mi alma. Gané en cinco duros sets.

WW *¿Qué es lo que más has aprendido de ti en este último año?*

NL Que cuando me fijo objetivos pongo todo de mí para poder alcanzarlos. También he aprendido que nunca estoy satisfecho, quiero alcanzar más logros y estoy dispuesto a hacer los sacrificios que sean necesarios para conseguirlo.

---

www.miwebworks.com.

WW *¿Qué tipo de cancha es tu preferida?*

NL Diría que las canchas de arcilla, pero este año han sido las canchas de cemento.

WW *¿Quiénes son tus ídolos del tenis?*

NL Ivan Lendl y Andrés Gómez.

WW *¿Quién fue tu primer entrenador?*

NL Mi papá, él me dio las primeras lecciones. Le agradezco por eso.

WW *¿Finalmente a qué edad le pudiste ganar a tu papá?*

NL Le gané cuando tenía 12 ó 13 años.

WW *¿Qué aspecto de tu juego consideras que es el mejor?*

NL Mi forehand siempre ha sido la mejor parte de mi juego.

WW *¿Y qué aspecto consideras como el más débil?*

NL El próximo año quisiera mejorar la devolución del servicio.

WW *¿Tienes alguna cábala?*

NL Sí. Cuando llego a un camerino, uso la misma ducha durante todo el torneo.

WW *¿Qué parte de tu entrenamiento es la que menos disfrutas?*

NL Mi entrenador le llama El Mortal. Consiste en lo siguiente: Él se pone en la net con una canasta de pelotas y por los siguientes tres minutos me tiene corriendo por toda la cancha, sin parar y a toda velocidad. Si lo piensas, tres minutos no es mucho tiempo, pero durante El Mortal parece una eternidad.

WW *¿Qué te gustaría decirles a tus fans?*

NL Gracias por todo su apoyo durante este año. Sólo les puedo retribuir trabajando cada vez más fuerte para darles más buenas noticias el próximo año.

EJERCICIOS

RECOGNIZING THE INFLUENCE OF ENGLISH

A Complete the following exercise.

1 Write the English words that appear in the selection.

____________________ ____________________

____________________ ____________________

____

2 Write the Spanish adaptation of the word "ranked" that appears in the first paragraph of the selection. ____________________

USING COGNATES TO DETERMINE MEANING

B Match each Spanish word in the first column with the English word in the second column that has the same meaning.

1 _____ *reforzar*	a	coach
2 _____ *mortal*	b	return
3 _____ *entrenador*	c	speed
4 _____ *iluminar*	d	news
5 _____ *devolución*	e	deadly
6 _____ *noticias*	f	willing
7 _____ *prolongarse*	g	disappoint
8 _____ *dispuesto*	h	intensify
9 _____ *velocidad*	i	light up
10 _____ *decepcionar*	j	lengthen

Beware of false cognates. Following are Spanish words with their true English meaning.

emocionante	exciting
sensible/impulsivo	emotional

C Complete the following sentences.

1 *El jugador es una persona muy* ______________________. (emotional)

2 *El jugador es una persona muy* ______________________. (exciting)

3 *El jugador hizo una decisión* ______________________. (emotional)

USING WORD FORMATION TO DETERMINE MEANING

D Many verbs have related noun forms. Write the English meaning of the following nouns.

	VERB		NOUN	
1	*lograr*	to achieve	*el logro*	____________
2	*luchar*	to struggle	*la lucha*	____________
3	*alcanzar*	to reach	*el alcance*	____________
4	*reforzar*	to reinforce	*el refuerzo*	____________
5	*apoyar*	to support	*el apoyo*	____________

USING CONTEXT TO DETERMINE MEANING

E Consider the context in which each of the following words and phrases appears in the selection, then write the English meaning of each.

1 *atrasado* ____________________

2 *su infaltable gorra* ____________________

3 *el Abierto* ____________________

4 *extenuado* ____________________

5 *hinchas* ____________________

6 *canchas de arcilla* ____________________

7 *le agradezco* ____________________

8 *cábala* ____________________

9 *camerino* ____________________

UNDERSTANDING DISCOURSE MARKERS AND OTHER EXPRESSIONS

F Read the following sentences and write the English meaning of the word or phrase that appears in bold type.

1 ***además***

a *Su hermano es un chico inteligente, guapo y* ***además****, muy simpático.*

____

b *Es muy atlético. Juega tenis, voleibol y* ***además****, fútbol.*

____

c *Le importa mucho su entrenamiento. Juega al tenis todos los días y* ***además****, corre diez kilómetros cada domingo.* ____________________

2 ***por supuesto***

a *El tenista hablaba de todo, de su familia, de sus amigos, de sus estudios y* ***por supuesto****, de su pasión por el tenis.* ____________________

b *Cuando volvió a la ciudad llamó a todos sus familiares, a sus amigos y* ***por supuesto****, a su novia.* ____________________

3 ***cada vez más***

a *La chica está enferma. No come nada y está* ***cada vez más flaca****.*

____

b *El atleta practica todos los días y está* ***cada vez más fuerte****.*

____

c *Tenemos que trabajar* ***cada vez más duro****.* ____________________

Fútbol centroamericano: a la conquista del mundo

Desde hace un buen tiempo, Centroamérica exporta jugadores a las distintas ligas del mundo. Ya no es raro escuchar de estrellas de esta región militando en la Liga Mexicana. Desde que se instauró, la liga mayor de fútbol de los Estados Unidos (MLS), ha puesto sus ojos en esta parte del continente americano. Pero ahora, se están comenzando a escuchar nombres como Paulo César Wanchope u Oscar David Suazo, triunfando en tierras europeas.

Este éxodo de jugadores centroamericanos, no solamente ha ayudado a las economías de los propios jugadores, a sus familias y equipos, sino que también colabora en buena medida para que el fútbol regional se cotice mejor.

Los dirigentes de los equipos europeos ya no sólo miran para Argentina, Brasil y Uruguay. Saben, desde hace un buen tiempo, que en Centroamérica se practica buen fútbol y que por ahora les puede salir más barato traerse a uno que la toque como David Suazo, para luego venderlo al mejor postor. Al fin y al cabo esto es un negocio.

Echaremos un vistazo a las figuras de esta región que triunfan en el extranjero.

El resumen a continuación demuestra esta participación en una temporada reciente.

NOMBRE	EQUIPO
Guatemala	
Dwight Pezzarossi	Palestino/Chile
Carlos "El Pescadito" Ruiz	Pas Iaonnina/Grecia
Guillermo "El Pando" Ramírez	Pas Iaonnina/Grecia
El Salvador	
Mauricio Cienfuegos	Galaxy/Los Angeles EEUU
Raúl Ignacio Díaz Arce	Mutiny/Tampa Bay EEUU
Jorge "Zarco" Rodríguez	Burn/Dallas EEUU
Ronald Zerritos	ADET

Renán Cardona, en *Acción Deportiva,* 14 de agosto de 2001, pp. 20–21.

NOMBRE	EQUIPO
Honduras	
Oscar David Suazo	Juventus de Turín/Italia
Carlos Pavón Plummer	Udinese/Italia
Iván Guerrero	Coventry City/Inglaterra
Jairo Martínez	Coventry City/Inglaterra
Eduardo "El Balín" Bennett	Argentinos Juniors/Argentina
Milton "Tyson" Núñez	Uruguay
Francisco Pavón	Badbleiberg/Austria
Reynaldo Clavasquín	Badbleiberg/Austria
Julio César Suazo	Badbleiberg/Austria
Walter Nahun López	Badbleiberg/Austria
Juan Manuel Cárcamo	Salzburgo/Austria
Maynor Suazo	Salzburgo/Austria
Amado Guevara	Toros Neza/México
"Ninrod" Medina	Saltillo/México
Alex Pineda Chacón	Fusion/Miami EEUU
Costa Rica	
Paulo César Wanchope	Manchester City/Inglaterra
Hernán Medford	Necaxa/México
Jafet Soto	Tecos azteca/México
Reynaldo Parks	Tecos azteca/México
Ronald Gómez	OFI-Creta/Grecia
Wilson Muñoz	OFI-Creta/Grecia
William Sunsing	New England Revolution/EEUU
Mauricio Wright	New England Revolution/EEUU
Alexander Madrigal	La Piedad, México
Mauricio Solís	Earthquakes/San José EEUU
Panamá	
Armando Dely Valdés	Sub-20/España
Julio César Dely Valdés	Málaga/España
Felipe Baloy	Envigado/Colombia

EJERCICIOS

USING COGNATE AND CONTEXT SKILLS TO DETERMINE MEANING

A Write the Spanish equivalent of the following words and phrases.

Sustantivos

1	league	________	6	exodus	________
2	star player	________	7	economy	________
3	region	________	8	family	________
4	part	________	9	business	________
5	continent	________			

Adjetivos

1	different	________	3	European	________
2	unusual	________	4	regional	________

Verbos

1	to export	________	4	to collaborate	________
2	to battle	________	5	to play (practice)	________
3	to triumph	________			

UNDERSTANDING TIME AND DISCOURSE EXPRESSIONS

An activity that began at some time in the past and is still occurring is usually expressed by the present or present progressive tense. Certain expressions are used with these tenses to give specific time information.

***Hace** cinco años **que** vivo aquí.*	I have been living here for five years.
*Vivo aquí **desde hace** cinco años.*	I have been living here for five years.
*Vivo aquí **desde** 1990.*	I have lived here since 1990.
***Desde que** vivo aquí, juego en este equipo.*	Ever since I have lived here, I have played on this team.

B Answer the following questions.

1 How long has Central America been exporting players?

____

2 How long has the MLS been looking toward this area for players?

____

Certain expressions indicate relationships between phrases.

no... sino indicates a correction

No *es del Salvador,* ***sino*** *de Honduras.*	He's **not** from El Salvador; he**'s** from Honduras.

no solamente..., sino también not only . . . , but also

Carlos ***no*** *es* ***solamente*** *buen jugador,* ***sino también*** *buen embajador.*	Carlos is **not only** a good player, **but also** a good ambassador.

ya now/already/finally

Despiértate, niño, ***ya*** *estamos en casa.*	Wake up, child, we're home **now**.
—Mamá, ¿cuando vamos a llegar a casa?	Mom, when are we going to get home?
*—****Ya*** *estamos aquí, hijo.*	We're **already** here, son.
¡Qué bueno que ***ya*** *estamos aquí!*	Thank goodness we're **finally** home!

al fin y al cabo when all is said and done/after all

C Write the English equivalent of the following sentences.

1 *Ya estamos en el estadio. Vamos a ver el partido.*

____

2 *"El Pescadito" no es de El Salvador, sino de Guatemala.*

____

3 *Los jugadores no son solamente buenos, sino también más baratos.*

____

4 *Hace ya tres años que su hijo es futbolista profesional.*

____

5 *Pasa el día entero hablando de fútbol. Al fin y al cabo, es su trabajo.*

____

Tres historias

Gol de Martino

Fue en 1946. El club uruguayo Nacional iba venciendo al argentino San Lorenzo y cerraba sus líneas de defensa ante las amenazas de René Pontoni y Rinaldo Martino. Estos jugadores habían ganado fama haciendo hablar a la pelota y tenían la mala costumbre de meter goles.

Martino llegó al borde del área. Allí se puso a pasear la pelota. Parecía que tenía todo el tiempo del mundo. De pronto Pontoni cruzó como rayo hacia la punta derecha. Martino se detuvo, alzó la cabeza, lo miró. Entonces los defensas de Nacional se echaron en masa sobre Pontoni, y mientras los galgos perseguían a la liebre, Martino entró en el área como Perico por su casa, eludió al zaguero que quedaba, tiró y fulminó.

El gol fue de Martino, pero también fue de Pontoni, que supo despistar.

Gol de Puskas

Fue en 1961. El Real Madrid enfrentaba, en su cancha, al Atlético de Madrid.

No bien comenzó el partido, Ferenc Puskas metió un gol bis, como había hecho Zizinho en el Mundial del 50. El atacante húngaro del Real Madrid ejecutó una falta, al borde del área, y la pelota entró. Pero el árbitro se acercó a Puskas, que festejaba con los brazos en alto:

—*Lo lamento* —se disculpó—, *pero yo no había pitado.*

Y Puskas volvió a tirar. Disparó de zurda, como antes, y la pelota hizo exactamente el mismo recorrido: pasó como bola de cañón sobre las mismas cabezas de los mismos jugadores de la barrera y se coló, como el gol anulado, por el ángulo izquierdo de la meta de Madinabeytia, que saltó igual que antes y no pudo, como antes, ni rozarla.

Eduardo Galeano, *El fútbol a sol y sombra*, Siglo XXI Editores, S.A. de C.V., pp. 95, 128 y 160.

Gol de Maradona

Fue en 1973. Se medían los equipos infantiles de Argentinos Juniors y River Plate, en Buenos Aires.

El número 10 de Argentinos recibió la pelota de su arquero, esquivó al delantero centro del River y emprendió la carrera. Varios jugadores le salieron al encuentro: a uno se la pasó por el jopo, a otro entre las piernas y al otro lo engañó de taquito. Después, sin detenerse, dejó paralíticos a los zagueros y al arquero tumbado en el suelo, y se metió caminando con la pelota en la valla rival. En la cancha habían quedado siete niños fritos y cuatro que no podían cerrar la boca.

Aquel equipo de chiquilines, *Los Cebollitas*, llevaba cien partidos invicto y había llamado la atención de los periodistas. Uno de los jugadores, *El Veneno*, que tenía trece años, declaró:

—*Nosotros jugamos por divertirnos. Nunca vamos a jugar por plata. Cuando entra la plata, todos se matan por ser estrellas, y entonces vienen la envidia y el egoísmo.*

Habló abrazado del jugador más querido de todos, que también era el más alegre y el más bajito: Diego Armando Maradona, que tenía doce años y acababa de meter ese gol increíble.

Maradona tenía la costumbre de sacar la lengua cuando estaba en pleno envión. Todos sus goles habían sido hechos con la lengua afuera. De noche dormía abrazado a la pelota y de día hacía prodigios con ella. Vivía en una casa pobre de un barrio pobre y quería ser técnico industrial.

EJERCICIOS

RECOGNIZING POETIC DEVICES

Consider the following examples of artistic expression in these three selections.

haciendo hablar a la pelota	"making the ball talk"
cruzar como rayo	"to cross (the field) like lightning"
los galgos perseguían a la liebre	"the greyhounds went after the hare"
como Perico por su casa	"like Perico entering his own house"
como bola de cañón	"like a cannonball"
habían quedado 7 niños fritos	"seven boys were fried"

USING COGNATES, CONTEXT, AND WORD FORMATION TO DETERMINE MEANING

A Answer the following questions about the first selection, *Gol de Martino.*

1 *¿Qué año era?* ____________

2 *¿Qué equipos jugaban?*

____

3 *¿Quiénes estaban ganando al principio?* ____________________

4 *¿Para qué equipo jugaban Pontoni y Martino?* ____________________

5 *¿Cuál era su "mala costumbre"?* ____________________

6 *¿Quién tenía la pelota al borde del área?* ____________________

7 *¿Qué hizo Pontoni para despistar al otro equipo?*

____

8 *¿Qué hicieron los defensas de Nacional?* ____________________

9 *¿Quién metió el gol?* ____________________

B Answer the following questions about the second selection, *Gol de Puskas.*

1 *¿Cuándo fue el partido?* ____________

2 *¿Quiénes jugaban?* ____________________

3 *¿Quién hizo el primer gol, y para qué equipo jugaba?*

____

4 *¿De qué nacionalidad era este jugador?* ____________________

5 *¿Por qué no aceptó el gol el árbitro?* ____________________

6 *¿Qué pasó después?* ____________________

C Answer the following questions about the third selection, *Gol de Maradona.*

1 *¿Cuándo y dónde fue el partido?* ____________________

2 *¿Quiénes jugaban?* ____________________

3 *¿Qué número tenía el chico que hacía milagros con la pelota?* ____________

4 *¿Cuántos partidos llevaba invicto el equipo Los Cebollitas?* ____________

5 *¿Quién dijo que nunca jugarían por dinero?* ____________________

6 *¿Quién hizo el gol increíble?* ____________________

7 *¿Qué quería ser este chico?* ____________________

El cine y el teatro

Películas en cartel

La vida prometida

(Est-Ouest). Francia. 1999. 1 h. 50 m. Alta Films. Drama. Dir. Régis Wargnier. Con Sandrinne Bonnaire, Catherine Deneuve y Oleg Ménshikov.
La difícil adaptación de una mujer francesa a la vida en la Rusia de la que procede su marido poco después de la Segunda Guerra Mundial. Estuvo nominada al Oscar a la mejor película extranjera, pero sucumbió ante el "efecto Almodóvar". 7 años.
Princesa (V.O. en francés sub.)

Pásate a la pasta

Ita.-Esp. 1999. UIP. 1 h. 39 m. Comedia. Dir. Antonello de Leo. Con Pere Ponce, Claudia Gerini y Ana Risueño.
El editor de una sofisticada revista mantiene una apasionada relación con su novia, una feminista radical que canta en un conjunto punk. Pero sus respectivos mundos chocan demasiado como para que las mentiras con que ocultan su verdadera condición puedan durar.
Ábaco, Bristol, Lido, Morasol, Palacio de la Prensa, AMC 24, Estrella.

Todo sobre mi madre

España. 1999. 1 h. 30 m. Warner Sogefilms. Drama. Dir. Pedro Almodóvar. Con Cecilia Roth, Marisa Paredes y Penélope Cruz.
Cuando un chaval muere en manos de su madre tras haber sido atropellado, la mujer decide ir a buscar al padre del chico para contarle que, años atrás de su relación nació el niño que ahora ha muerto. El mayor éxito de Almodóvar, que ha arrasado en los Goya, ganado el premio de mejor director en Cannes y el Globo de Oro, ha rematado su triunfo con el ansiado Oscar a la Mejor Película Extranjera. 18 años.
Acteón, Aluche, Estación de Chamartín La Dehesa (Sólo 19.30 h), ***Estrella*** (Sólo 22.30 h).

Solas

España. 1998. 1 h. 38 m. Nirvana. Drama. Dir. Benito Zambrano. Con María Galiana, Ana Fernández y Carlos Álvarez.
Hermoso, honesto y sorprendente debut de Benito Zambrano, que pese a lo modesto de

Guía del ocio de Madrid, 14–20 de abril de 2000.

su producción se ha visto reconocido con cinco premios Goya. La agridulce relación de una madre que lo da todo y su hija, en permanente enfado con el mundo por la miseria que le ha tocado vivir, sirve al director para dar una lección de humildad y maestría. 13 años.
Estación de Chamartín
La Dehesa (Sólo 22.30 h),
Real Cinema, Renoir Plaza de España, Las Provincias.

Tarzán

EEUU. 1999. 1 h. 23 m. Buena Vista. Animación. Dir. Kevin Lima y Chris Buck.
Uno de los mitos literarios más frecuentados por el cine es la historia del cachorro humano criado entre gorilas que se convierte en una suerte de superhombre capaz de dominar a los demás animales, pero que deberá descubrir el modo de relacionarse con los propios humanos. Como fondo, la magnífica banda sonora creada por Phil Collins. Autorizada.
Albufera Yelmo Cineplex,
UGC Ciné Cité.

El mar

España. 1999. 1 h. 51 m. Lauren. Drama. Dir. Agustí Villaronga. Con Roger Casamajor, Ángela Molina y Simón Andreu.
Mallorca, 1936. Dos niños que tienen diez años cuando la Guerra Civil llega a la isla descubren el horror al ser testigos del fusilamiento de unos hombres. La espiral del odio que se genera no tardará en arrastrarlos a un mundo que les arrebata la inocencia.
Renoir Retiro, Rosales.

EJERCICIOS

SCANNING FOR INFORMATION

A Answer the following questions.

1 Which of these movies were not produced in Spain?

____________________ ____________________

2 Which movie is a collaboration between Spain and another country?

____

What country? ____________________

3 Which of these movies are appropriate for a ten-year-old child?

____________________ ____________________

4 Which movie doesn't give an age guideline, but is probably okay for a ten-year-old? ______________________

5 Which theaters are showing two of the movies in this guide?

______________________ ______________________

6 What time can you see *"Todo sobre mi madre"* at Estación de Chamartín La Dehesa Theater? ______________________

7 Which of these movies were nominated for an Oscar?

______________________ ______________________

8 What other awards were won by these movies?

______________________ ______________________

____

9 What is a *banda sonora*? ______________________

Which of these movies has a highly acclaimed one?

____

10 Which of these movies have war themes? What wars are depicted?

____

____

USING COGNATES TO DETERMINE MEANING

B Write the English equivalent of the following words.

***Sustantivos* (Nouns)**

1 *drama* ______________

2 *comedia* ______________

3 *efecto* ______________

4 *triunfo* ______________

5 *miseria* ______________

6 *mito* ______________

7 *historia* ______________

8 *isla* ______________

9 *horror* ______________

10 *espiral* ______________

11 *inocencia* ______________

12 *humildad* ______________

13 *director* ______________

14 *editor* ______________

15 *feminista* ______________

16 *gorila* ______________

17 *animal* ______________

18 *adaptación* ______________

19 *relación* ______________

20 *condición* ______________

21 *producción* ______________

22 *lección* ______________

Adjetivos (Adjectives)

1	*difícil*	________	9	*humano*	________
2	*radical*	________	10	*capaz*	________
3	*respectivos*	________	11	*magnífica*	________
4	*honesto*	________	12	*sofisticada*	________
5	*modesto*	________	13	*apasionada*	________
6	*permanente*	________	14	*reconocido*	________
7	*literario*	________	15	*nominada*	________
8	*frecuentado*	________			

Verbos (Verbs)

1	*sucumbir*	________	5	*dominar*	________
2	*ocultar*	________	6	*descubrir*	________
3	*servir*	________	7	*relacionar(se)*	________
4	*convertir(se)*	________	8	*generar*	________

Beware of false cognates. Following are Spanish words with their true English meaning.

éxito	success
salida	exit
suceso	event

C Complete the following sentences.

1 *Vi a una amiga mía en la* ________ *del teatro.*
exit

2 *La gala de los Oscar fue el* ________ *del año.*
event

3 *La película tuvo mucho* ________.
success

Solas

Una película de Benito Zambrano

Sinopsis

En un barrio pobre y conflictivo de una gran ciudad, madre e hija se ven obligadas a convivir. María, la hija, embarazada de un hombre que no quiere saber nada de ella, malvive limpiando.

El vecino de arriba es un viejo huraño que vive con su perro Aquiles.

La madre, pese a las dificultades que pasan, se empeñará en romper la dureza de María y cambiarla con su dulzura. También querrá terminar con la soledad del vecino. Su mensaje es claro: sólo el amor puede ayudarles a atravesar con dignidad el largo túnel de sus vidas.

El director

Nacido en Lebrija (Sevilla) en 1965, Benito Zambrano se licenció en guión y dirección por la Escuela Internacional de Cine y Televisión de San Juan de los Baños (La Habana, Cuba). En 1995, presentó su mediometraje *El encanto de la luna llena,* recibido con aplausos y premios en los festivales de Friburgo (Suiza), Huesca, Museum of Contemporary Art (Sydney, Australia), entre otros.

Solas es su ópera prima. Presentada en la Sección Panorama del reciente Festival de Berlín, ha conseguido una mención CICAE (Crítica Internacional) y una mención especial del Jurado Ecuménico, formado por las organizaciones eclesiásticas protestantes y católicas. Prensa y público apoyaron la apuesta valiente de esta película que narra el encuentro y el desencuentro de una madre y una hija en un entorno conflictivo. El film, en su estreno, parte como rotunda ganadora.

El equipo

Los escasos cien millones de pesetas que ha costado *Solas* no andan parejos con la incuestionable calidad del film, como ha sido reconocido en el Festival de Berlín, 1999. Sevilla es el escenario principal de

Cine Renoir, Cine Princesa, Madrid.

esta historia de perdedores fotografiada por Tote Trenas, brillante iluminador de películas desde 1986. Uno de los músicos que colabora en *Solas* es el guitarrista Tomatito, que acompaña a la cantante Neneh Cherry en la canción *Woman* de la banda sonora original de la película. La actriz principal es Ana Fernández (María en *Solas*). Sevillana de nacimiento, Ana Fernández, hasta ahora, ha sido una de las voces más importantes del doblaje español. También se ha destacado en el film *Yerma* y en otras producciones de cine, teatro y televisión. Éste es su primer papel protagonista. María Galiana (la madre en *Solas*) es una actriz que ha trabajado con buena parte de los mejores directores del cine español. *Solas* es su primer papel estelar. Carlos Álvarez-Novaa, también sevillano como sus compañeras, es un actor con mayor experiencia en el teatro.

EJERCICIOS

USING WORD FORMATION TO DETERMINE MEANING

Sometimes a prefix is added to a verb to give it a more specific meaning.

sobre + *vivir*	→ *sobrevivir*
over to live	to survive

A Find two verbs in the selection that feature *vivir* with a prefix, then write the verbs and the English meaning of each.

1 ______________________ ______________________

2 ______________________ ______________________

The prefix *des-* can indicate an opposite meaning.

VERB		NOUN	
aparecer	to appear	*la aparición*	the appearance
desaparecer	to disappear	*la desaparición*	the disappearance
esperar	to hope	*la esperanza*	the hope
desesperar	to despair	*la desesperanza*	the despair

B Find the following words in the selection, then write the meaning of each.

1 *el encuentro* ______________________

2 *el desencuentro* ______________________

The suffix *-eza* may be added to an adjective to describe its essence. The resulting form is a feminine noun.

sutil	subtle	*la sutileza*	the subtlety
gentil	kind	*la gentileza*	the kindness

C If *duro* means "hard/tough," what does *la dureza* mean?

____

The suffix *-ura* may also be added to an adjective to describe its essence. The resulting form is a feminine noun.

amargo	bitter	*la amargura*	the bitterness
tierno	tender	*la ternura*	the tenderness

D Following the *-ura* pattern, write the noun corresponding to each of the following adjectives.

1 *hermoso* ______________________

2 *gordo* ______________________

3 What does *la dulzura* mean? ______________________

E Find the nouns in the selection that correspond to the following words in English, then answer the questions that follow.

1 loneliness ______________________

2 city ______________________

3 dignity ______________________

4 quality ______________________

5 difficulty ______________________

6 What suffix do they all have? ____________

7 What gender are they? ______________________

F Find the nouns in the selection that correspond to the following words in English, then answer the questions that follow.

1 direction (theatrical) ______________________

2 television ______________________

3 mention ______________________

4 song ______________________

5 production ______________________

6 What suffix do they all have? ____________

7 What gender are they? ______________________

El guión ("script," from *guiar* "to guide") is masculine, like *el avión* ("airplane").

G Write the Spanish equivalent of each verb below. Then find the noun in the selection that designates a person whose job or lifestyle involves each activity, and write both the masculine and feminine nouns.

	VERB	NOUNS
1 to win	______________	______________________
2 to lose	______________	______________________
3 to do the lighting	______________	______________________
4 to direct	______________	______________________

5 What suffix do these words use to indicate a male? ___________

a female? ___________

RECOGNIZING FALSE COGNATES

Following are Spanish phrases with their true English meaning.

estar embarazada	to be pregnant
tener vergüenza	to be embarrassed

H Complete the following sentences.

1 *Su madre* ________________________ *de su gordura.*
is embarrassed

2 *Su madre* ________________________.
is pregnant

USING CONTEXT TO DETERMINE MEANING

I Read each sentence, then write the meaning of the word(s) that appear in bold type.

1 *Madre e hija* ***se ven*** *obligadas a convivir.* ______________________

2 *Es un viejo* ***huraño*** *que vive con su perro.* ______________________

3 *La madre* ***se empeñará*** *en romper la dureza de su hija.*

____

4 *Van a* ***atravesar*** *el largo túnel de sus vidas.* ______________________

5 *La madre y la hija viven en un* ***entorno*** *conflictivo.*

____

6 *La película es* ***rotunda*** *ganadora.* ______________________

7 *El* ***estreno*** *de su nueva película será el próximo mes.*

____

8 *La voz de Ana Fernández es una de las más importantes del* ***doblaje*** *de las películas extranjeras en España.* ______________________________

9 *La actriz* ***juega el papel*** *de la hija en esta película.*

____

10 *La película dura una hora, es un* ***mediometraje****.*

____

Todo sobre mi madre

En el año 1999 Pedro Almodóvar recibió en Hollywood el Óscar por la mejor película extranjera, titulada "Todo sobre mi madre". A continuación está la sinopsis de esta película.

Un refrán griego dice que sólo las mujeres que han lavado sus ojos con lágrimas pueden ver con claridad. El refrán no se cumple con Manuela. La noche que un coche atropelló a su hijo Esteban, Manuela lloró hasta quedar totalmente seca. Y lejos de ver con claridad, el presente y el futuro se confunden en la misma oscuridad.

Esa misma noche, mientras espera en el hospital, lee las últimas líneas que su hijo ha escrito en un bloc de notas del que nunca se separa. "Esta mañana busqué en la habitación de mi madre hasta encontrar un fajo de fotos. A todas les faltaba la mitad. Mi padre, supongo. Tengo la impresión de que a mi vida le falta ese mismo trozo. Quiero conocerlo, no me importa quién sea, ni cómo se haya portado con mamá. Nadie puede quitarme ese derecho...."

Nunca le dijo quién era: "Tu padre murió mucho antes de que tú nacieras" fue lo máximo que Manuela llegó a decirle. En memoria de su hijo, Manuela abandona Madrid y va a Barcelona a buscar al padre. Quiere decirle que las últimas palabras que su hijo escribió iban dirigidas a él, aunque no lo conociera. Pero antes debe decirle al padre, que cuando ella lo abandonó hace 18 años iba embarazada, y que tuvieron un hijo, y que este hijo acaba de morir. También le dirá que le puso de nombre Esteban, como él, su padre biológico antes de que cambiara su nombre.

Manuela va a Barcelona en busca del padre de su hijo. La búsqueda de un hombre que ha cambiado de nombre no puede resultar sencilla. Y en efecto no lo es.

Cine Renoir, Cine Princesa, Madrid.

EJERCICIOS

USING COGNATES TO DETERMINE MEANING

A The following English words and expressions have Spanish cognates. Find the Spanish equivalents in the selection and write them in the space provided.

Sustantivos

1 synopsis ________________
2 refrain ________________
3 the present ________________
4 the future ________________
5 hospital ________________
6 line ________________
7 note ________________
8 the impression ________________
9 in memory of ________________

Adjetivos

1 entitled ________________
2 biological ________________

Verbos

1 he received ________________
2 they get confused ________________
3 he doesn't separate himself from ________________
4 to encounter ________________
5 she abandoned him ________________
6 to result ________________

Adverbios

1 totally ________________

RECOGNIZING FALSE COGNATES

abandonar can mean "to abandon" when it is followed by a noun referring to a person, but it means "to leave" when it is followed by the name of a place

continuación can mean "continuation," but *a continuación* means "coming up next"

embarazada looks like "embarrassed," but it means "pregnant" ("to be embarrassed" is *tener vergüenza* or *tener pena*)

en efecto looks like "in effect," but it means "indeed" or "as a matter of fact"

oscuridad looks like "obscurity," but it means "darkness"

última looks like "ultimate," but it means "final" or "last"

B Complete the following sentences.

1 *Mucha gente* ____________ (leaves) *la ciudad en el verano porque hace mucho calor.*

2 *Es muy difícil ver bien en la* ____________ (darkness).

3 *Después de* ____________ (abandoning) *a su esposo, ella descubrió que estaba* ____________ (pregnant).

4 *Vamos a Madrid la* ____________ (last) *semana en mayo.*

5 *Un concierto de música moderna viene* ____________ (coming up next).

6 *La profesora* ____________ (is embarrassed) *de su error.*

7 *La segunda novela es* ____________ (a continuation) *de la primera.*

USING A SPANISH-SPANISH DICTIONARY TO FIND MEANING

C The following Spanish words in bold type do not have English cognates, but their definitions contain words that have English cognates. Using these clues, write the English meaning of each item.

1 ***la película*** *el filme/imágenes cinematográficas* ____________

2 ***la mujer*** *persona de sexo femenino* ____________

3 ***seca*** *sin agua, sin jugo, sin humedad* ____________

4 ***trozo*** *fragmento* ____________

5 ***quitar*** *separar* ____________

6 ***sencilla*** *sin dificultad* ____________

USING WORD FORMATION TO DETERMINE MEANING

Imperfect subjunctive forms are made from the third-person plural preterite forms by subtracting the *-on* and adding *-a*, etc.

hablaron *habla**ra***
comieron *comie**ra***
tuvieron *tuvie**ra***

These forms follow expressions like *antes de que* and *aunque (no)* when they refer to past action.

antes de que fuera abogado before he was a lawyer
antes de que vendiera su casa before she sold her house
antes de que compraras ese coche before you bought that car

antes de que dijera la verdad	before she told the truth
aunque trabajara en la ciudad	even though he worked in the city
aunque no hablara español	even though he didn't speak Spanish
aunque siempre comiera sola	even though she always ate alone
aunque saliera todas las noches	even though she went out every night

D The following imperfect subjunctive clauses are taken from the selection; write their English meaning in the space provided.

1 *aunque no lo conociera* ______________________________

2 *antes de que tú nacieras* ______________________________

3 *antes de que cambiara su nombre* ______________________________

REREADING FOR COMPREHENSION

E Read the article again, then answer the following questions.

1 What prize did this movie win? ______________________________

2 What was the mother's name? ______________________

3 What was the son's name? ______________________

4 What was the father's real name? ______________________

5 Where did the mother go in order to find the father?

____

6 Was it easy for her to find him? ___________

7 Does this movie appeal to you? ___________

Carlos Saura

El más destacado y reconocido director español, Carlos Saura, nació en 1932. Estudió periodismo y cine antes de realizar su primera cinta, el corto *"Cuenca"*. Rápidamente se movió hacia la vanguardia del cine español. Su obra incluye *"El jardín de las delicias"*, *"Cría cuervos"*, la trilogía *"Bodas de sangre"*, *"Carmen"*, *"El amor brujo"*, *"Sevillanas"*, *"Taxi"* y *"Tango"*.

Saura regresa a la gran forma demostrada en su extraordinaria trilogía flamenca con una glamorosa y refinada producción, una película que ha titulado sencillamente *"Flamenco"*. Este gran espectáculo de flamenco es de 100 minutos de duración y comienza con una actuación espontánea de un grupo de cantaores, bailaores y músicos que expresan sus sentimientos a través de la música y de sus cuerpos. A partir de este impresionante principio, Saura captura unas maravillosas interpretaciones que van desde el ballet y lo clásico a lo popular y hasta lo experimental, lo narrativo y lo pantomímico. Hombres, mujeres, jóvenes, viejos, fandango, tango, tarantelas: todos están representados en este extraordinario film.

Saura combina todos los recursos teatrales, musicales y cinematográficos a su disposición. Pantallas en blanco, espejos y luces de colores crean el efecto de una travesía músico-visual desde el atardecer hasta el amanecer. *"Flamenco"* es una de las grandes películas de Saura y uno de los mejores films de baile de todos los tiempos.

---

www.flamenco-world.com.

EJERCICIOS

USING COGNATES TO DETERMINE MEANING

A The following English words have cognates that appear in the selection. Write the Spanish equivalent of the English words.

Sustantivos

1	director	____________	7	the acting	____________
2	short (film)	____________	8	group	____________
3	vanguard/ avant-garde	____________	9	feeling/ sentiment	____________
4	trilogy	____________	10	music	____________
5	production	____________	11	interpretation	____________
6	length/ duration	____________	12	resource	____________

Adjetivos

1	extraordinary	____________	5	impressive	____________
2	glamorous	____________	6	of the theater	____________
3	refined	____________	7	of music	____________
4	spontaneous	____________	8	blank	____________

Verbos

1	move	____________	5	capture	____________
2	include	____________	6	represent	____________
3	commence	____________	7	combine	____________
4	express	____________			

Adverbio

1 rapidly ____________

USING WORD FORMATION TO DETERMINE MEANING

The construction *lo* + masculine singular adjective expresses the essence of the adjective as an abstract noun.

lo difícil	what is difficult
lo interesante	what is interesting

B The Spanish equivalent of the following phrases can be found in the selection. Write them in the space provided.

1 what is classic ____________________

2 what is popular ____________________

3 what is experimental ____________________

4 what is narrative ____________________

5 what is like pantomime ____________________

USING CONTEXT AND COGNATES TO DETERMINE MEANING

C Each word in the first column appears in the selection. Consider its context there, then match it with the most appropriate expression in the second column.

1 _____ *destacado* a *video*

2 _____ *periodismo* b *cristal que refleja*

3 _____ *cinta* c *jornada*

4 _____ *baile* d *la parte del televisor donde aparecen las imágenes*

5 _____ *pantalla* e *danza*

6 _____ *espejo* f *extraordinario*

7 _____ *travesía* g *escritura*

UNDERSTANDING EXPRESSIONS

D The English expression "from sunup to sundown" can be expressed in Spanish as *durante todo el día* or *desde el amanecer hasta el atardecer.*

Write the words in the selection that mean *"durante toda la noche."*

____

Yo nunca quise ser escritor

Cuando terminaba sus estudios de periodismo en la Universidad de Chile, Alberto Fuguet descubrió, casi sin darse cuenta, su afinidad con la literatura. «Quería escribir como no me dejaban hacerlo mis profesores», dice. Publicó muy pronto *Sobredosis,* su primer libro de cuentos, y desde entonces se apartó un poco del periodismo y de la crítica de cine—una de sus pasiones—para dedicarse a la escritura, incluso, de guiones cinematográficos. Publicó con éxito las novelas *Mala onda* y *Por favor, rebobinar*. El año pasado se estrenó en Chile la película *En un lugar de la noche,* basada en un guión suyo, y hace pocos meses se presentó en Santiago *Tinta roja,* largometraje dirigido por Francisco Lombardi (*Pantaleón y las visitadoras*), basado en la novela homónima de Fuguet. Esta película relata, como en el libro, la vida de Alfonso, un periodista que termina trabajando en *El Clamor,* un diario sensacionalista de Santiago.

SEMANA *¿En qué momento dio el salto del periodismo a la literatura?*

ALBERTO FUGUET Yo nunca quise ser escritor. Me imagino que después tomé esa decisión porque el periodismo no me daba lo que yo quería que me diera. Yo, de chico, aparte de ser bombero quería ser periodista y, sobre todo, crítico de cine porque, además, era la manera que me parecía más fabulosa de ver películas gratis. Pero escritor como tal no. Yo leía más revistas y diarios que libros. Fue terminando la escuela de periodismo que recién se me ocurrió escribir, no antes. Mis primeros cuentos los escribí como para compensar esa "pirámide invertida" que nos inculcaban en la universidad.

SEMANA *¿Por qué se alejó de la crítica de cine cuando publicó su primer libro?*

AF Para mí las películas son iguales que los libros, son más difíciles, creo yo, y más caras. Me daba miedo atacar a alguien y sentir que esa persona podía ser herida como yo. Por eso me alejé de la crítica. Ahora, 10 años después, he vuelto con una columna semanal en el diario *El Mercurio*. Y está bueno, no las puedo ver antes sino que las veo con el público. Algo que he concluido con mi jefe es que los críti-

---

Semana, 27 de agosto de 2001, pp. 72–73. Reproducida aquí con el permiso de *Semana Magazine,* Colombia.

cos son personas extrañas. Con *Tinta roja,* un amigo mío que es crítico me dijo sobre el estreno: estuvo helado. Sí, así, frío. Y después me di cuenta que era una opinión de crítico. Este año que estoy escribiendo de cine no puedo ver las películas con los críticos, las veo con el público. Es lo mejor para no hacer esos comentarios.

SEMANA *¿Qué directores de cine admira?*

AF A todos. Me gusta el cine en general. Depende del estado de ánimo. No me gusta lo que se llama "artista-artista" en el que uno tiene que mentir a la salida del teatro, posando de intelectual. En general me siento más norteamericano. En una época amé a Brian de Palma. Me encantan Truffaut, Spielberg, Woody Allen.

SEMANA *¿'Tinta roja' la escribió pensando en una posible película?*

AF Totalmente. Cada capítulo era como una escena. Había un plano general y después me iba a los diálogos. Con *Tinta roja,* aparte del mundo policial, yo quería que un estudiante de periodismo también se identificara. Pero el libro no es "antiperiodismo" ni "antiperiodismo amarillo". Es casi celebratorio. Hay una cosa que me enseñó mi jefe verdadero y que está en la novela: *"No se te olvide nunca que siempre alguien te va a leer".*

SEMANA *¿Le gustó la versión cinematográfica de 'Tinta roja'?*

AF Lombardi es un cineasta bueno. El libro está muy bien resumido. Yo sé que no es el libro. La adaptación es bastante más conservadora de lo que yo la hubiera hecho. La película es más romántica que el libro. Se filmó en Lima y a los chilenos eso les molestó. Yo estoy muy contento porque la calidad de los actores es muy buena.

EJERCICIOS

RECOGNIZING FALSE COGNATES

Following are Spanish words with their true English meaning.

la salida	the exit
con éxito	successfully
los sucesos	the events

A Complete the following sentences.

1 *Vamos a* ______________________ *del teatro.* (the exit)

2 *Vamos a recapitular* ______________________ *de la tarde.* (the events)

3 ______________________ *de la pieza nos sorprendió.* (The success)

USING WORD STUDY TO DETERMINE MEANING

Consider the formation and meaning of the following Spanish words.

criticar	verb	to criticize
crítica	adjective	critical, referring to *una crisis,* as in *una situación crítica*
la crítica	noun	the opinion/the writing of reviews
el crítico/la crítica	noun	the critic, reviewer

B Complete the following sentences.

El ____________ (critic/reviewer) *fue duro con la película.* ____________ (He criticized) *la dirección, la actuación y la escenografía. Esperamos que* ____________ (the opinion) *del público sea más favorable. Yo no quisiera dedicarme a* ____________ (the writing of reviews).

USING WORD FORMATION TO DETERMINE MEANING

The word *se* has a number of uses in Spanish. It may be used with a verb in the third person to give more emphasis to the action than to the actor.

Se estrena la película el jueves. The movie is being shown for the first time on Thursday.

C In the selection, find the *se* construction with the verb in the past tense, then write the Spanish equivalent of the following sentence.

The movie was shown for the first time in Chile last year.

____

D Write the English equivalent of the following sentences.

1 *La película se presenta la próxima semana.*

____

2 *La película se presentó la semana pasada.*

____

3 *Se filmó la película en Lima.*

____

Se attached to the end of an infinitive indicates a verb that must always be used with a reflexive pronoun.

dedicarse	*Me dedico a mis estudios.*	I spend a lot of time studying.
	Se dedica a su trabajo.	He is devoted to his job.
	Tiene tiempo para dedicarse al trabajo.	He has time to devote himself to his job.

alejarse	to distance oneself/get away from
apartarse	to leave/drop/abandon
darse cuenta de	to realize

E The following sentences appear in the selection. Write their English equivalent.

1 *Se apartó del periodismo y de la crítica para dedicarse a la escritura.*

____

2 *Por eso me alejé de la crítica.*

____

3 *Y después me di cuenta que era una opinión de crítico.*

____

Se can be followed by an indirect object pronoun with certain verbs that indicate unplanned occurrences.

Se me olvidó.	I forgot. (It didn't enter my head.)
Se le ocurrió...	It occurred to him . . .
Se me perdió el boleto.	I lost the ticket. (The ticket got lost.)

F The following sentences appear in the selection. Write their English equivalent.

1 *Fue terminando la escuela que se me ocurrió escribir.*

____

2 *"No se te olvide nunca que siempre alguien te va a leer".*

____

Compare the imperfect and preterite meanings of the verb *querer*.

No quería estudiar; quería salir.	I didn't want to study; I wanted to go out. (That is what I wanted to do at the time.)
Quise estudiar, pero no pude.	I tried to study (during that entire period of time), but I didn't manage to do it.
Nunca quise estudiar.	I didn't want to study (during that entire period of time), and I didn't.

No quise estudiar.	I never intended to study./I refused to study.

G In the following sentences, tell whether the action is being described **during the period** in the past or **after it is over**.

1 *Quería escribir como no me dejaban mis profesores.* ______________

2 *No quise ser escritor.* ______________

3 *El periodismo no me daba lo que yo quería.* ______________

USING CONTEXT TO DETERMINE MEANING

H Read the following sentences, then write the meaning of the words that appear in bold type.

1 *Tomó mucha medicina y sufrió una* ***sobredosis****.* ______________

2 *Después de ver el video, tienes que* ***rebobinarlo****.* ______________

3 *¿Estás enfermo? ¡Qué* ***mala onda****!* ______________

4 *Si me gusta la película depende del* ***estado de ánimo****. Si estoy de buen humor, me gusta; si estoy de mal humor, no me gusta.* ______________

I Find words in the selection that correspond to the following English expressions and write them below.

1 yellow journalism ______________

2 "arty" ______________

SKIMMING FOR GENERAL MEANING

J Reread the entire interview quickly, then answer the following questions.

1 Where is Alberto Fuguet from, and what does he do?

____

2 What are his two separate—but related—professions?

______________ ______________

3 What newspaper does he work for? ______________

4 Who are some of the filmmakers he admires?

______________ ______________

______________ ______________

5 What type of film does he dislike the most? ______________

6 How did he feel about the movie *Tinta roja*?

____

Fundación Arlequín Teatro

Temporada 2001

"Willy y nosotros"

Escenas de amor, humor y muerte del inmortal William Shakespeare, entrelazadas con canciones sobre sus sonetos, serán interpretadas por María Elena Sachero y José Luis Ardissone y cantadas por Ricardo Flecha. Pasarán así la escena del balcón de "Romeo y Julieta", la muerte de Desdemona de "Otello", y escenas de "La fierecilla domada", "Hamlet" y "Sueño de una noche de verano". La dramaturgia y dirección serán de José Luis Ardissone y las canciones serán compuestas por Jorge Garbett y Jorge Krauch.

"Abran cancha que aquí viene Don Quijote de la Mancha"

Sobre la obra cumbre de la literatura española, la autora Adela Basch ha escrito esta deliciosa comedia musical para niños y adolescentes. Con música de Jorge Krauch y dirección de Erenia López, la obra reunirá en el elenco a jóvenes figuras del arte escénico. El estreno está previsto para el mes de julio.

"El médico a palos"

Del inmortal Molière, la Fundación Arlequín Teatro escogió la divertida comedia "El médico a palos". Esta obra es un baile de máscaras, donde todos pretenden ser lo que no son. El autor nos presenta a un falso médico, una falsa enfermera, un falso boticario, un falso amor paterno. Y los que no juegan un papel carnavalesco, juegan el papel de crédulos. Esta obra de Molière es una evidente sátira social. Lo sorprendente en ella es que ninguno de los personajes, por lo tanto, ninguno de los grupos que ellos representan, se libra de su pluma mordaz. En el rol del "médico" estará el actor Juan Carlos Cañete, y los demás roles serán cubiertos por Alejandra Ardissone, Julio Saldaña, Rossanna Schembori, María José Cacavelos, Osvaldo Lapuente, Monchi Delvalle, Nelson Aguilera, Armando Gómez y Enrique Vera. El estreno está previsto para el mes de julio.

Algunas Obras Presentadas

2000

"Palma... del Petit Boulevard al Lido bar" de José Luis Ardissone
"El espectáculo que nos ofrece Arlequín es para el gusto de toda la familia, nos divierte con humor y nos emociona sin dramatismo, nos invita a mirarnos y a reflexionar sobre nosotros mismos como sociedad".—Gloria Muñoz

1998

"La tierra sin mal" de Augusto Roa Bastos
"Un monumento teatral a la primicia de la conciencia del hombre, un tema, un autor y una actuación que hacen honor al Paraguay, a su historia y a su gente".—Mons. Lorenzo Baldisseri

1993

"¡Ay, Carmela!" de José Sanchis Sinisterra
"¡Ay, Carmela! es un trabajo sólido, rico y apasionado".—Jorge Aiguadé

1983

"La casa de Bernarda Alba" de Federico García Lorca
"Al cerrarse el telón uno queda sumergido en una sensación de deseo satisfecho, de admiración por una labor que merece el agradecimiento más profundo".—Noemí Nagy

EJERCICIOS

SCANNING FOR DETAILS

A Answer the following questions.

1 What plays are featured for the 2001 season?

____________________ ____________________

____

2 Which of these plays could you take a group of children to?

____

3 Which of these plays are based on the work of authors who are no longer living?

____________________ ____________________

____________________ ____________________

4 Which ones are musicals?

______________________ ______________________

5 Which one is a social satire? ______________________

6 Which ones will be presented in the month of July?

______________________ ______________________

7 For at least how long has this theater been operating? ______________

8 Who is probably the director of this theater? ______________________

9 Who is probably in charge of the music? ______________________

10 Of all the plays mentioned in this program, which one is about Paraguay? Who wrote it?

____

USING CONTEXT TO DETERMINE MEANING

B Write the English meaning of the words that appear in bold type.

1 *Escenas de amor, humor y muerte del inmortal William Shakespeare,* ***entrelazadas*** *con canciones sobre sus sonetos...*

____

2 Don Quijote de la Mancha*, la obra* ***cumbre*** *de la literatura española...*

____

3 *La obra reunirá en el* ***elenco*** *a jóvenes figuras del arte escénico.*

____

4 *Los que no juegan el papel* ***carnavalesco****, juegan el papel de* ***crédulos****.*

______________________ ______________________

5 *Al cerrarse el* ***telón****, uno queda sumergido en una sensación de deseo...*

____

PERU

El fabricante de deudas

por Sebastián Salazar Bondy

Personajes Jacinto, *mayordomo. Edad mediana. Simpático y locuaz.*
Luciano Obedot, *el falso rico. 50 años. Tiene muchas virtudes, pero muchos más defectos.*
Godofreda, *cocinera. Vieja.*
Jobita, *sirvienta. Joven.*

Entra, apresurado, Obedot.

OBEDOT —¡Jacinto! ¡Llama por teléfono, de mi parte, al señor Obeso y ruégale que venga, de inmediato, a verme por un asunto extremadamente delicado! ¡Pon mucho énfasis en eso de "extremadamente delicado"! (*Pausa.*) ¡Corre! (*Cuando Jacinto va a hacerlo.*) ¡No olvides el whisky y el champán francés! (*Jacinto le interroga con la mirada y la actitud.*) ¡Arréglate como puedas! ¡Corre!

JACINTO —Haré lo que esté en mis manos hacer... (*Sale.*)

OBEDOT —(*A Jobita.*) Tú, anda inmediatamente con el chofer a las mismas tiendas a las que llevó a la señora anteayer y diles a los vendedores que te entreguen inmediatamente el pedido. Las cuentas serán pagadas en la casa, al contado, a la sola presentación de las facturas.

JOBITA —Sí, señor. (*Va a salir. Se detiene.*) ¿Y si se niegan?

OBEDOT —Insiste, insiste. Que venga contigo un empleado para pagarle aquí mismo en dinero contante y sonante.

JOBITA —Sí, señor. (*Vuelve a detenerse.*) ¿Y la gasolina para el auto?

OBEDOT —(*Irritado.*) ¡Que la pague el chofer! ¡No le han de faltar unos soles en el bolsillo!

JOBITA —Bien, señor... (*Sale amedrentada.*)

OBEDOT —(*Entusiasta.*) ¡Y tú, Godofreda, hoy tienes que hacer milagros con las ollas! Se sentará a nuestra mesa esta noche el Marqués de Rondavieja. Estarán también el distinguido señor don Bernardo Torrecillas, y el señor y la señora Obeso. Siete en total.

GODOFREDA —(*Tímida.*) Pero, señor...

Carlos Solórzano, *El teatro hispanoamericano contemporáneo; antología*, pp. 205–7.

OBEDOT —¡Vuela! ¡No hay tiempo que perder!

GODOFREDA —Pero el verdulero, el carnicero, nadie quiere...

OBEDOT —(*Intimidante.*) ¿Nadie quiere qué?

GODOFREDA —Nadie quiere vendernos al crédito ni siquiera una lechuguita.

OBEDOT —(*Seguro.*) Eso no es problema. Acude a los competidores de esos malos comerciantes. En el país reina el libre comercio.

GODOFREDA —Pero, ¿cómo les pagaré, señor?

OBEDOT —Abre cuentas en sus almacenes... (*Ante un gesto escéptico de la mujer.*) Inspírales confianza, que eso franquea las puertas del crédito.

GODOFREDA —(*Vacilante.*) Lo intentaré, señor. (*Va hacia la puerta. Antes de salir.*) ¡No puedo pagarles con mi plata, lo lamento!

OBEDOT —(*Va como un rayo hacia ella.*) Godofreda, Godofreda, en el régimen liberal el crédito es toda la riqueza. Si los pequeños comerciantes de este barrio desconocen tan simple y sabio principio económico, practicado aún por nuestro Supremo Gobierno en sus complejas finanzas, es que son unos ignorantes. (*Pausa.*) O, tal vez, unos pérfidos comunistas. (*Pausa.*) Y si tú los encubres, también serás sospechosa de comunismo.

GODOFREDA —(*Alarmada.*) Yo no, señor... (*Se persigna.*) Ellos, quizá, pero yo jamás.

OBEDOT —(*Con tono tranquilo.*) Además, si a la postre los proveedores resultan enemigos del orden público y te exigen dinero, dales sin temor del tuyo. Te haré ganar buenos intereses. Diez soles semanales por cada cien de inversión. ¿Te parece bien? Es mucho mejor interés que el de la Caja de Ahorros, ¿no es cierto?

GODOFREDA —(*Cayendo en la trampa.*) ¿La Caja de Ahorros? ¡Bah, una miseria, señor!

OBEDOT —(*Triunfal.*) ¿Y cómo es posible, mujer, que sirviendo en mi casa, trabajando en el hogar de un hábil financista, entregues tu dinero a manos agiotistas e inescrupulosas? ¡En adelante, yo seré tu Caja de Ahorros! ¡10% semanal de intereses!

GODOFREDA —(*Ganada por la codicia.*) ¿Es cierto eso, don Luciano?

OBEDOT —En este asunto no soy tu empleador. Soy tu socio.

GODOFREDA —(*Contenta.*) ¡Oh, gracias, señor! ¡Hoy comerá usted manjares celestiales! (*Sale corriendo.*)

EJERCICIOS

SKIMMING FOR MEANING

A Read the entire selection quickly, then answer the following questions.

1 Of the four characters in this scene, who are the two most important?

____

2 How does Obedot treat his employees? ____________________

3 Is Obedot an honorable man? ____________

4 What does he try to trick Godofreda into doing? ____________________

USING WORD FORMATION TO DETERMINE MEANING

Command forms in Spanish depend on whether you are addressing a person as *tú* (familiar) or *usted* (formal). *Tú* commands are formed as follows.

Affirmative commands

Drop the *-s* from the present indicative *tú* form.

llama call   *corre* run   *abre* open

Add any object pronouns to the end of the verb.

*ruéga**le*** beg him   *inspíra**les*** inspire (in) them

Be aware of irregular forms in common verbs.

di tell/say   *pon* put   *haz* do   *sal* leave

Negative commands

Use the following formula.

no + object pronoun(s), if any + subjunctive form ending in *-s*

no lo compres don't buy it
no los comas don't eat them
no lo abras don't open it

B Find the commands in the selection and write them below.

1	____________	8	____________
2	____________	9	____________
3	____________	10	____________
4	____________	11	____________
5	____________	12	____________
6	____________	13	____________
7	____________	14	____________

USING CONTEXT TO DETERMINE MEANING

C The words *el pedido, las facturas,* and *unos soles* may be unfamiliar to you; however, you can probably guess their meaning when you read them in context. Write the English meaning of the words that appear in bold type.

1 *La señora fue a las tiendas anteayer. Hoy van los empleados para recoger* ***el pedido****.* ____________________

2 *No puedes cambiar lo que compraste si no tienes* ***la factura****.*

____

3 *La señora le pagó diez* ***soles*** *por el periódico.* ____________________

D Find an expression in the selection that means "cold, hard cash" and write it in the space below.

____

USING A SPANISH-SPANISH DICTIONARY

E The following words from the selection do not give hints as to their English meaning; however, their Spanish-only dictionary definitions in the second column will help you—and introduce you to new words at the same time. Write the English meaning of each Spanish word.

1 ***amedrentada*** *intimidada* ____________________

2 ***encubrir*** *ocultar* ____________________

3 ***franquear*** *abrir/hacer posible* ____________________

4 ***manjares*** *platos deliciosos* ____________________

5 ***codicia*** *avaricia* ____________________

6 ***socio*** *compañero en negocios* ____________________

7 ***jamás*** *en ninguna ocasión* ____________________

UNDERSTANDING HUMOR

F What do you suppose the name "Sr. Obeso" means here?

____

REREADING FOR GREATER UNDERSTANDING AND ENJOYMENT

G Reread the entire selection, then answer the following questions.

1 *¿Quién es el señor Obedot?*

____

2 *¿Cómo trata a sus empleados?* ____________________

3 *¿Qué le pide a Jacinto que haga?*

____

4 *¿Qué le ordena a Jobita que haga?*

____

5 *Según Obedot, ¿quién puede pagar la gasolina?* ____________________

6 *¿Qué van a hacer esta noche?*

____

7 *¿Quién es el invitado de honor?* ______________________________

8 *¿Cuántas personas estarán en la cena?* _______________

9 *Según Obedot, ¿adónde puede ir Godofreda para comprar los comestibles?*

____

10 *Según Obedot, ¿quién puede pagar si no aceptan crédito?*

____

11 *¿Qué pretende el señor Obedot?*

____

12 *¿Cae en la trampa Godofreda?* _________________________

El arte

Museos

Museo Nacional Villaroy

Ubicado en el distrito de Buenos Aires, en Tegucigalpa. Está abierto de miércoles a domingo, de las 8:30 hasta las 15:30 horas. Guarda arqueología precolombina, colonial, historia natural y muestras etnográficas.

Museo Histórico de la República

La antigua casa presidencial de Honduras es ahora un museo donde se exhibe parte de la historia del país, desde la Independencia de España. Ubicado en el centro de la ciudad capital, antigua casa presidencial de Tegucigalpa, abierto de martes a sábado, de las 9:00 hasta las 12:00 horas y de las 13:30 hasta las 16:00 horas.

Sala Bancatlán

Una valiosa colección privada de objetos prehispánicos, monedas y pinturas de los artistas contemporáneos más importantes de Honduras. Ubicada en la Plaza Bancatlán, en el bulevar Miraflores en Tegucigalpa. Abierto de lunes a viernes, de las 9:00 hasta las 15:00 horas.

Museo del Hombre

Ubicado en la Avenida Cervantes, en el antiguo edificio donde estuvo la Corte Suprema de Justicia en el centro de Tegucigalpa. Este museo exhibe una serie de objetos que muestran la evolución del hombre, además de contar con un antiguo cuarto de restauración de pintura.

El Museo de Antropología e Historia de San Pedro Sula

Invita a todas las familias sampedranas y de ciudades vecinas a disfrutar de un fin de semana diferente visitando las diversas salas en las que se exponen sus valiosas colecciones prehispánicas y coloniales.

---

www.123.hn/Museos.htm.

EJERCICIO

SCANNING FOR INFORMATION

A Answer the following questions.

1 Which of these museums are museums themselves—of historic architecture?

____

____

2 Where could you go to see contemporary Honduran paintings?

____

3 Which of these museums have collections of pre-Columbian art?

____

____

____

4 Which of these museums is not located in the capital city of Honduras?

____

5 Which museum could you visit at noon on a weekday, but not on Sunday?

____

El arco iris

por Rufino Tamayo

A Olga

Azul como el hondo mar cuando está tranquilo,
verde como el campo en tiempo de lluvia,
naranja como puesta de sol en el otoño,
violeta como reflejo carmesí sobre el mar azul,
magenta como las bugambilias
que adornan nuestros jardines,
ocre como la tierra erosionada de la altiplanicie,
café como la tierra húmeda de fértil trópico,
rosa como conjunción del sol y la luna,
gris como mañana sin sol en día lluvioso,
amarillo como tierno sol en día de primavera,
blanco como el color de la luna llena,
negro como noche sin luna y sin estrellas,
rojo como el fuego que todo lo consume.

EJERCICIO

UNDERSTANDING ARTISTIC DEVICES IN LITERATURE

In this poem, one of Mexico's best-known and most-respected painters uses **simile** to paint his colors. In similes, Spanish *como* corresponds to English "like."

A Read the poem carefully, then answer the following questions in Spanish.

What color . . .

1 is the sea when it's still? ____________________

2 is the countryside during the rainy season? ____________________

3 is the autumn sunset? ____________________

Mario Mijango, *El otro Tamayo*, Editorial Diana 2000.

4 is the reflection of the sea? ____________________

5 are the bougainvilleas? ____________________

6 is the land of the high plains? ____________________

7 is the humid, fertile land of the tropics? ____________________

8 is the combination of the sun and the moon? ____________________

9 is a sunless, rainy day? ____________________

10 is the sun in springtime? ____________________

11 is the full moon? ____________________

12 is a moonless, starless night? ____________________

13 is the fire that consumes it all? ____________________

El muralismo mexicano

El muralismo mexicano nació a finales de la década de 1920, cuando el gobierno decidió poner a disposición de los artistas el espacio mural de los edificios públicos. Fue así que los pintores más entusiasmados por una revolución social, sobre todo Diego Rivera, José Clemente Orozco y David Alfaro Siqueiros, trajeron el arte a la gente común. Estos pintores declararon su desprecio por el arte de los círculos ultraintelectuales y aristocráticos, y se dedicaron al arte "monumental"—un arte que sería propiedad de toda la gente.

El movimiento del monumentalismo tenía como meta resaltar y engrandecer la revolución y la historia del país. Sus temas eran la vida del mexicano común, sus valores y costumbres y la lucha social. Este arte existía para propagar ideas y expresarlas clara y sobriamente.

La belleza de la obra de los muralistas se encuentra en su simplicidad, su vitalidad y su originalidad en capturar, con colores fuertes y formas grandes, el sabor de México y esos momentos de su historia.

EJERCICIOS

SKIMMING FOR MEANING

A Read the selection quickly, then answer the following questions.

1 What country's best-known art is described here? ______________________

2 When did the painting of murals on public walls begin there?

____

USING COGNATES TO DETERMINE MEANING

B Find the words in the selection that are cognates of the English words below and write them in the space provided.

Nouns (*Sustantivos*)

1	artist	__________	9	history	__________
2	circle	__________	10	idea	__________
3	color	__________	11	moment	__________
4	custom	__________	12	movement	__________
5	decade	__________	13	painter	__________
6	disposition	__________	14	revolution	__________
7	form	__________	15	space	__________
8	government	__________	16	value	__________

Adjectives (*Adjetivos*)

1	mural	__________	5	common	__________
2	public	__________	6	ultra-intellectual	__________
3	enthusiastic	__________	7	aristocratic	__________
4	social	__________			

UNDERSTANDING WORD FORMATION

The suffix *-idad* indicates a feminine noun; it is often added to an adjective to express its essence.

especial — *la especialidad*
feliz — *felicidad*

C Write the noun that is formed from each of the following adjectives.

1 *vital* __________
2 *original* __________
3 *creativo* __________
4 *genial* __________

A noun ending in *-ismo* indicates a movement involving a group of people with a common interest. An individual member of that group, male or female, is identified by the suffix *-ista.*

el muralista	the male muralist
la muralista	the female muralist

D Following the same pattern, write the missing forms below.

	MOVEMENT	INDIVIDUAL MEMBER
1	*el socialismo*	____________
2	*el monumentalismo*	____________
3	*el cubismo*	____________
4	____________	*el/la surrealista*
5	*el expresionismo*	____________
6	____________	*el/la futurista*
7	*el impresionismo*	____________
8	*el modernismo*	____________

Actions that began and ended in the past are expressed by the preterite tense. Third-person endings in this tense for most verbs are as follows.

USTED/ÉL/ELLA	*USTEDES/ELLOS/ELLAS*
-ó/-ió/-o	*-aron/-ieron/-eron*

Preterite forms of the verb *ir* ("to go") are as follows.

fue	*fueron*

E Find the preterite verbs in the selection that correspond to their English cognates below and write them in the space provided.

1 decided ____________

2 declared ____________

What do the following words mean?

3 *capturó* ____________

4 *propagaron* ____________

5 *expresaron* ____________

USING CONTEXT TO DETERMINE MEANING

F Read the following sentences, then write the meaning of the words that appear in bold type.

1 *El muralismo mexicano* ***nació*** *a finales de la década de 1920.*

____

2 *Los muralistas* ***trajeron*** *el arte a la gente común.* ______________________

3 *Estos pintores* ***se dedicaron*** *al arte "monumental".* ______________________

4 *El arte monumental es* ***propiedad*** *de toda la gente.* ______________________

5 *La* ***meta*** *del gobierno es tranquilizar a la gente.* ______________________

6 *La meta del arte fue* ***resaltar*** *y* ***engrandecer*** *la revolución.*

______________________ ______________________

7 *Uno de los temas fue la* ***lucha*** *social del mexicano común.*

____

READING FOR COMPREHENSION

G Read the entire selection again, then answer the following questions.

1 What was the purpose of the first mural painting in Mexico?

____

2 Who were the most important artists?

______________________ ______________________

____

3 What is "monumental art"?

____

4 What distinguishes these mural paintings?

____

Frida Kahlo

Magdalena Carmen Frida Kahlo y Calderón nació el 6 de julio de 1907 en Coyoacán, México, hija de padre alemán de origen húngaro y de madre mexicana. Una niña ya sensible e introspectiva, a los seis años sufrió un ataque de poliomielitis, que la dejó traumatizada y con una pierna malformada. Había sido antes vivaz y sociable, una niña que jugaba fácilmente tanto con los niños de su vecindad como con sus hermanas y sus primos. De repente se encontró aislada, mandada al exilio de su habitación de enferma. Estaba muy sola y tenía que aprender sola a centrarse. Aunque tenía una relación muy estrecha con su padre, él tenía que trabajar y no podía dedicarle el tiempo que ella necesitaba. Su madre, con otras dos niñas en la casa, tampoco tenía mucho tiempo para atenderla, así que, además del dolor terrible de su pierna derecha, tenía que soportar la soledad y el dolor psicológico de la enfermedad. Esta enfermedad la dejó con cicatrices tanto físicas como mentales.

Cuando era joven, Frida usaba pantalones para ocultar su pierna malherida. Más tarde, la escondía debajo de hermosas faldas largas, típicas de la ropa indígena mexicana.

Frida sufrió otras desgracias.

A la edad de 19 años, resultó muy herida en un accidente de tránsito: tenía rotas la columna vertebral, la clavícula, dos costillas, la pierna y el pie derechos y encima, la pelvis fracturada y el hombro dislocado.

En 1929 se casó con el pintor Diego Rivera—un genio intrigante y ya exitoso, pero también un hombre viejo, gordo, mujeriego, dos veces divorciado y padre de tres hijos. A su lado vivió maravillas, alegrías, torturas y sufrimientos que sólo se pueden imaginar de un matrimonio poco convencional de dos personas poco convencionales. Lo cierto es que juntos compartieron una gran amistad, un amor profundo, la alegría de vivir, una dedicación al arte y una preponderante pasión por México.

Frida Kahlo supo transferir todos los elementos de su ser—su belleza, su fragilidad, sus sufrimientos, sus alegrías, sus tormentas y sus pasiones—a todos sus proyectos. Nos ha regalado una obra no solamente conmovedora, sino magnífica por su expresión intensamente humana.

EJERCICIOS

SKIMMING FOR MEANING

A Read the entire selection quickly, then answer the following questions.

1 What nationality is Frida Kahlo? ____________________

2 Who was her husband? ____________________

USING WORD FORMATION TO DETERMINE MEANING

The suffix *-mente* indicates an adverb that describes how an action is performed. Such an adverb is often formed by adding *-mente* to the feminine form of an adjective.

maravillosa	*maravillosamente*
completa	*completamente*
inteligente	*inteligentemente*

B Using the same pattern, write the adverb that is formed from each of the following adjectives.

1 *introspectiva* ____________________

2 *sociable* ____________________

3 *feliz* ____________________

4 *psicológica* ____________________

5 *terrible* ____________________

6 *física* ____________________

7 *mental* ____________________

8 *profunda* ____________________

9 *preponderante* ____________________

10 *intensa* ____________________

The suffix *-ado/-ido* indicates the past participle form of the verb. This form is often used as an adjective to describe a noun by a completed action.

traumatizar to traumatize   *traumatizado* traumatized

C Using the verb on the left, write a past participle to describe each noun on the right. Keep in mind that adjectives (including past participles) always agree in gender and number with the nouns they describe.

1 *traumatizar*   *una niña* ____________________

2 *malformar*   *una pierna* ____________________

3 *aislar*   *un hombre* ____________________

4 *herir* — *unos hombres* ____________________

5 *fracturar* — *el brazo* ____________________

6 *dislocar* — *el tobillo* ____________________

7 *divorciar* — *una mujer* ____________________

8 *romper* (irregular participle: *roto*) — *la clavícula* ____________________

RECOGNIZING FALSE COGNATES

Following are Spanish words with their true English meaning.

aislar	to sequester
secuestrar	to kidnap
sensato	sensible
sensible	sensitive

D Complete the following sentences.

1 *La niña era muy* ____________________ (sensitive).

2 *El jefe es un hombre muy* ____________________ (sensible).

3 *Intentaron* ____________________ (kidnap) *a varias personas.*

4 *Ella estaba* ____________________ (sequestered) *en su cuarto durante largos períodos.*

READING FOR COMPREHENSION

E Read the entire selection again, then answer the following questions.

1 When was Frida Kahlo born? ____________________

2 What are the origins of her last names?

____

3 What was she like as a child? ____________________

4 What two things caused her physical suffering?

____

5 How did she like to dress?

____

6 What was her married life like? ____________________

7 What is the most important quality of her work?

____

Pablo Picasso

Pablo Ruiz Picasso, pintor y escultor español, oriundo de la isla de Málaga, es considerado por muchos uno de los artistas plásticos más importantes del siglo XX. Fue único y genial en todas sus facetas: inventor de formas, innovador de técnicas y estilos, artista gráfico y escultor. Con más de 20.000 trabajos, fue uno de los creadores más prolíficos de toda la historia.

Es extraordinaria la dedicación a la pintura que tenía Picasso. Trabajaba como investigador científico, con paciencia y constancia. Su obra se destaca por su claridad, locura, gracia, pasión, arrebato, arbitrariedad y burla violenta. En toda esta obra imaginativa y maravillosa—sus dibujos, pinturas, esculturas, litografías—se ve el gran y alegre corazón del artista.

Dijo Picasso:

«Cada niño es un artista. El problema es ¿qué hacer para que siga siendo artista una vez que crezca?»

«Todos quieren entender la pintura. ¿Por qué no tratan de entender la canción de los pájaros?»

«Los ordenadores son inútiles, sólo te pueden dar respuestas.»

«Algo nuevo, algo que valga la pena hacer no puede ser reconocido. La gente simplemente no tiene tanta visión.»

«Dénme un museo y lo llenaré.»

«No existe el arte abstracto. Siempre es necesario empezar por algo. Después se pueden quitar todas las huellas de la realidad.»

«Todos sabemos que el arte no es la verdad. El arte es la mentira que nos hace conocer la verdad—por lo menos la verdad que nos es posible entender.»

«Los malos pintores copian. Los buenos roban.»

«Nada puede hacerse sin soledad. Es difícil hoy estar solo, porque tenemos relojes. ¿Habéis visto un santo con reloj?»

EJERCICIOS

SKIMMING FOR GENERAL MEANING

A Read the first two paragraphs of the selection quickly, then answer the following questions.

1 Who was Pablo Picasso? ______________________________

2 What country was he from? ____________________

USING CAREFUL OBSERVATION TO FORM OPINIONS

B Read the quotations from Picasso carefully, then answer the following questions.

1 Do you agree strongly with one of these statements in particular? Write the meaning of this statement and explain why you agree with it.

____

____

____

2 Do you disagree with any of these ideas? Write the meaning of the idea and explain why you feel this way.

____

____

____

READING FOR COMPREHENSION

C Read the entire selection again, then answer the following questions.

1 In what forms did Picasso express his art?

______________________ ______________________

______________________ ______________________

2 Why is he considered prolific?

____

3 What qualities distinguish his work?

______________________ ______________________

______________________ ______________________

______________________ ______________________

____

4 What is apparent in all of his work? ____________________________

Salvador Dalí

Salvador Dalí, pintor catalán, produjo entre los años 1929–1937 las pinturas que lo hicieron el pintor surrealista más famoso del mundo. En ellas, pintó un mundo soñado, en el cual los objetos corrientes se ven en yuxtaposición, deformados o metamorfoseados de una manera extraña e irracional. Estos objetos parecen aun más surreales porque los pintó con meticuloso detalle realista, casi siempre en paisajes vacíos y soleados que recuerdan su tierra natal, Cataluña. Dalí puso su huella en la cinematografía, colaborando con el director Luis Buñuel en la producción de dos películas surrealistas. A fines de los años 30, empezó a pintar en un estilo más académico, a consecuencia de que fue expulsado del movimiento surrealista. Luego hizo varios proyectos comerciales y exploró una variedad de materias que se centraron en su esposa, Gala, y en otros temas que variaban de lo erótico hasta lo religioso. En total, fue un genio capaz de proyectar su ingeniosidad en una variedad de formas plásticas. Hizo que la gente sonriera.

Dalí, en sus propias palabras:

Biografía de Dalí

«El verdadero pintor es aquel que es capaz de pintar escenas extraordinarias en medio de un desierto vacío. El verdadero pintor es aquel que es capaz de pintar pacientemente una pera rodeada de los tumultos de la historia».

Biografía de Gala

«Llamo a mi esposa Gala, Galuxka, Gradiva; Oliva, por lo oval de su rostro y el color de su piel: Oliveta, diminutivo de la oliva; y sus delirantes derivados: Olíueta, Oriueta, Buribeta, Burieueteta, Suliueta, Solibubuleta, Oliburibuleta, Ciueta, Liueta. También la llamo Lionette, porque cuando se enfada ruge como el león de la Metro-Goldwyn-Mayer».

---

www.dali-estate.org/esp/dali1.htm.

EJERCICIOS

SKIMMING FOR MEANING

A Read the first paragraph quickly, then answer the following questions.

1 Who was Salvador Dalí? ______________________

2 Where was he from? ______________________

USING WORD PATTERNS TO DETERMINE MEANING

The construction *lo* + masculine singular adjective expresses the essence of the adjective as an abstract noun.

Lo bueno *es que nos ha hecho sonreír.*	The good thing is that he made us smile.
Ella ha hecho ***lo imposible*** *para ayudarnos.*	She has done the impossible to help us.

B Write the English meaning of the following sentence.

Sus temas varían de lo erótico hasta lo religioso.

____

RECOGNIZING ARTISTIC EXPRESSION

C In his autobiography, what qualities does Dalí imply are necessary in a true painter?

____

____

Simile is an artistic device used to make comparisons.

Sus ojos brillan como las estrellas.	Her eyes shine like stars.
Es tan vivo como un zorro.	He is as sly as a fox.

Alliteration is the repetition of the same sound in successive words or syllables.

El agua ***c****antaba su* ***c****opla* ***c****orriendo...*

D How does Dalí use simile and alliteration in his biography of his wife? Is he an artist in more than one sense of the word?

____

____

____

READING FOR COMPREHENSION

E Read the entire selection again, then answer the following questions.

1 What part of Spain was Dalí from? ____________________

2 What is he best known for?

____

3 In what media besides painting was his surrealism expressed?

____________________ ____________________

4 What is the usual reaction to his work? ____________________

Fernando Botero

«¡Pero sí es el hombre que pinta las gordas!», grita una persona que pasa por la playa, y él, esbozando una sonrisa, alza la mano para saludar. Ese es Fernando Botero, un hombre tan importante que no deja de lado su sencillez. Habla con su acento "paisa" (de la región colombiana de Antioquia, donde nació), que no ha perdido a pesar del tiempo que lleva viviendo fuera de su país.

Cada año, y de manera religiosa, Fernando y su esposa, la escultora griega Sophia Vari, van a México a pasar una temporada de descanso, aunque según Botero, el concepto de descanso no existe para un artista. «Yo trabajo 10 horas al día, sin importar donde esté, ni qué día de la semana sea; para mí el trabajo es el mayor placer que existe».

«A los 18 años me fui a Europa en barco; era la primera vez que veía el mar. Ahí estudié Historia del Arte y aprendí las técnicas de los grandes maestros italianos. No tenía dinero. Recuerdo un día en París que me empezó a doler una muela, fui al dentista y dijo que salía más barato sacármela que ponerme una calza, así que me la arrancó».

De cómo y cuándo encontró su estilo, dice «El interés en el volumen está presente en la gran pintura, sobre todo en la del Renacimiento Italiano, que ha sido de gran influencia para mí». Añade que estudió las obras de Diego Rivera y José Clemente Orozco y que sintió gran afinidad por la expresividad y el manejo de volúmenes de éste último, «pero todo sucedió un día en que estaba dibujando una mandolina y le hice el hueco del centro como una pequeña marca. Inmediatamente vi el efecto que tuvo en el instrumento: se deformó, cambió de dimensión». Así nació su muy particular estilo "boteresco", donde el volumen juega un papel preponderante.

En su pintura, Botero no sigue los patrones de la moda, sino su propia concepción del arte, inspirado en la realidad latinoamericana y en los recuerdos de su infancia en Medellín. Este artista, que define su estilo como "realidad imaginaria", se resiste a aceptar que pinta

---

Adaptada de Adriana Dávila, "Fernando Botero en Zihuatanejo", *Quién*, 1 de julio de 2001, pp. 85–87.

gordas; según su explicación, lo que hace es tratar de crear la sensualidad a través de la forma y el volumen. «Exagero, pero no invento. En mis cuadros no hay nada imposible, sino improbable».

EJERCICIOS

USING CONTEXT TO DETERMINE MEANING

A Read each of the following sentences, then write the meaning of the words that appear in bold type.

1 a *Mi amigo me saluda, **esbozando** una sonrisa.* ____________________

  b ***esbozar*** ____________________

2 a ***Alza** la mano para saludar.* ____________________

  b ***alzar*** ____________________

3 *Sale más barato sacarle el diente que ponerle una **calza**.*

____

4 *Hice el **hueco** del centro de la mandolina como una pequeña marca.*

____

RECOGNIZING FALSE COGNATES

Following are Spanish words with their true English meaning.

resistirse a/negarse a/no querer	to refuse
resistirse a	to resist
resistir/aguantar/soportar	to bear/stand
apoyar	to support (physically or with facts)
sostener	to support (physically)
sustentar	to support (with facts)
mantener	to support (financially)

B Complete the following sentences.

1 *Mi hermana* ____________________ *las películas violentas.*
can't stand

2 *Mi hermana* ____________________ *mis decisiones.*
supports

3 *Mi hermana* ____________________ *los postres de chocolate.*
can't resist

4 *Mi hermana* ____________________ *que su amiga se mude a otra ciudad.*
refuses to accept

USING PATTERN FORMATION TO DETERMINE MEANING

The verb *llevar* followed by a gerund (*-ndo*) form indicates that an activity has been going on for a certain period of time.

Llevo cinco años viviendo en esta ciudad.	I've been living in this city for five years.
Llevan casi una hora hablando por teléfono.	They've been talking on the telephone for almost an hour.

C Following the same pattern, write the Spanish equivalent of the following sentences.

1 Botero has been living outside his country for some time.

____

2 She has been painting for twenty years.

____

3 We've been waiting for you for thirty minutes.

____

USING DISCOURSE MARKERS TO DETERMINE MEANING

a pesar de despite/in spite of

Botero no pierde su acento, ***a pesar del*** *tiempo que lleva viviendo fuera de su país.*	Botero doesn't lose his accent, **in spite of** the time he's been living abroad.
El hombre no se cansa, ***a pesar de*** *las horas que trabaja.*	The man doesn't get tired, **in spite of** the hours he's been working.

no... sino... corrects a negative statement

Botero ***no*** *es mexicano,* ***sino*** *colombiano.*	Botero is**n't** Mexican; he**'s** Colombian.
En sus cuadros ***no*** *hay nada imposible,* ***sino*** *improbable.*	In his paintings there is **nothing** that is impossible, **but** much that is improbable.

D Using *a pesar de* or *no... sino*, complete the following sentences.

1 *Ella no está contenta aquí,* ____________ *que tiene muchos amigos.*

2 *Ella no está contenta,* ____________ *triste.*

3 *Mi amigo no trabaja solamente aquí,* ____________ *en otro lugar también.*

4 *Mi amigo siempre sonríe,* ____________ *sus preocupaciones.*

5 *Carolina sigue estudiando,* ____________ *la dificultad de la materia.*

UNDERSTANDING IDIOMS

Most languages have expressions whose literal translation into other languages makes no sense; these are called "idioms" (*"modismos"* in Spanish).

jugar un papel	to play a part
escribir un trabajo	to write a paper

E Complete the following sentences.

1 *Madonna* ______________________ *de Evita en la película.*
plays the part

2 *Evita* ______________________ *importante en la historia de Argentina.*
plays a part

3 *Tengo que* ______________________ *sobre la historia de Argentina.*
write a paper

READING FOR COMPREHENSION

F Read the entire selection, then answer the following questions.

1 *¿De dónde es Fernando Botero?* ______________________

2 *¿Qué característica tienen muchos de los personajes de sus pinturas y esculturas?* ______________________

3 *Para Botero, ¿cuál es el mayor placer de la vida?* ______________________

4 *Cuando era joven y estudiaba en Europa, ¿era rico o pobre?* ______________

5 *¿Por cuál de los pintores mexicanos siente afinidad?*

____

6 *¿Cómo define Botero su estilo?* ______________________

ARGENTINA

A la manera de Frida Kahlo

por Gladys Ilarregui

A veces yo perdía los anteojos
y se me perdía el mundo o daba vueltas la página
y una lágrima me ablandaba la silla o solamente
estaba en medio de una habitación inmaculada
mientras mis riñones soltaban charcos de sangre
y la infancia se hundía con camisones sin florcitas
y pies rosados, y afuera, en la ventana la plaza
aparecía repleta de palomas.

yo hubiera olvidado el abecedario por una corona
de manos, de niños haciendo una ronda hasta que
el sol caía, no como una transfusión sino como un
sol cansado, hasta que las mamás volvían con sus
"se acabó el juego" y el juego terminaba inocente
sin muñecas rotas, sin piezas de mecano que se ausentan
con un "hasta mañana"...

Guía para perplejos, p. 41. Reproducida aquí con el permiso de la autora, gladys@iberoamerican.org.

EJERCICIOS

APPRECIATING POETRY THROUGH ANALYSIS AND REPETITION

A One of the functions of the imperfect tense in Spanish is to describe activities that occurred over and over. The following exercise is designed to help the reader sense the pain and aching monotony of this child's existence. Find the expression in the first half of the poem that corresponds to each of the following phrases in English, and write it in the space provided.

1 and a tear would make the chair seem softer

____

2 and I felt like I'd lost the whole world

____

3 or a page would turn

____

4 I would be in the middle of an immaculate room

____

5 and my childhood drowned in plain nightgowns and pink feet,

____

6 while my kidneys would spill puddles of blood

____

7 while outside, in the window, the plaza would be full of pigeons

____

8 Sometimes I lost my glasses

____

Now recreate the poem by rewriting the Spanish lines in their original order.

____

____

____

____

____

____

____

____

B Match each expression on the left with its English equivalent on the right.

1	______ *una corona de manos*	a	the game is over
2	______ *hacer una ronda*	b	holding hands in a circle
3	______ *muñecas rotas*	c	the ABCs
4	______ *se acabó el juego*	d	see you tomorrow
5	______ *piezas de mecano*	e	pieces of construction toys
6	______ *hasta mañana*	f	broken dolls
7	______ *que se ausentan*	g	dancing in a circle
8	______ *el abecedario*	h	that get lost

C Answer the following questions.

1 What was going on outside?

____

2 What would the child have been glad to forget if she could have joined the other children? ______________________________

ARGENTINA

Graffiti

por Gladys Ilarregui

Mi hermano como un jackson pollock de cuatro años
ilustró la casa con lápices de cera. Una escritura
que en New York hubieran considerado profética
porque los niños saben seguir el rastro del misterio,
de lo imposible, pero a esa altura del mundo
en un pequeño pueblo sobre el mapa, las circunvoluciones
de colores hicieron que mi hermano quedara castigado
tres días con sus noches, y al atardecer del cuarto,
recién entonces, se le permitió volver a la mesa.

EJERCICIO

A Read the entire selection, then answer the following questions.

1 *¿Quién es el pintor?* ______________________

2 *¿Cuántos años tiene?* ______________________

3 *¿Qué usa el niño para pintar?* ______________________

4 *¿Con quién se lo compara?* ______________________

5 *¿Qué saben hacer los niños?* ______________________

6 *¿Por cuánto tiempo quedó castigado este niño?*

____

Guía para perplejos, p. 44. Reproducida aquí con el permiso de la autora, gladys@iberoamerican.org.

La familia

El árbol familiar

Los García

El Sr. García **Pedro García Martínez** *don Pedro*	*La Sra. (de) García* **María González de García** *doña María*
el esposo de María	**la esposa** de Pedro
el padre de José y de Ana	**la madre** de José y de Ana
el suegro de Susana y de Raúl	**la suegra** de Susana y de Raúl
el abuelo de Luisa, Juan, Juana y Jorge	**la abuela** de Luisa, Juan, Juana y Jorge

Los García / Los Hernández

La Sra. (de) García **Susana Díaz de García**	*El Sr. García* **José García González**	*La Sra. (de) Hernández* **Ana García González**	*El Sr. Hernández* **Raúl Hernández Castro**
la nuera de Pedro y de María	**el hijo** de Pedro y de María	**la hija** de Pedro y de María	**el yerno** de Pedro y de María
	el hermano de Ana	**la hermana** de José	
la esposa de José	**el esposo** de Susana	**la esposa** de Raúl	**el esposo** de Ana
la cuñada de Ana	**el cuñado** de Raúl	**la cuñada** de Ana	**el cuñado** de José
la madre de Luisa y de Juan	**el padre** de Luisa y de Juan	**la madre** de Juana y de Jorge	**el padre** de Juana y de Jorge
la tía de Juana y de Jorge	**el tío** de Juana y de Jorge	**la tía** de Luisa y de Juan	**el tío** de Luisa y de Juan

Luisa García Díaz	**Juan García Díaz**	**Juana Hernández García**	**Jorge Hernández García**
la hija de Susana y de José	**el hijo** de Susana y de José	**la hija** de Ana y de Raúl	**el hijo** de Ana y de Raúl
la nieta de Pedro y de María	**el nieto** de Pedro y de María	**la nieta** de Pedro y de María	**el nieto** de Pedro y de María
la sobrina de Ana y de Raúl	**el sobrino** de Ana y de Raúl	**la sobrina** de Susana y de José	**el sobrino** de Susana y de José
la prima de Juana y de Jorge	**el primo** de Juana y de Jorge	**la prima** de Luisa y de Juan	**el primo** de Luisa y de Juan

EJERCICIOS

A Write the English equivalent of the following nouns.

1 *la suegra* ________________ 6 *la nuera* ________________

2 *el cuñado* ________________ 7 *los hermanos* ________________

3 *el sobrino* ________________ 8 *los tíos* ________________

4 *el yerno* ________________ 9 *los padres* ________________

5 *la nieta* ________________ 10 *los hijos* ________________

B Complete the following sentences in Spanish.

El hermano de mi padre es mi **(1)** ________________*; su esposa es mi* **(2)** ________________ *y sus hijos son mis* **(3)** ________________*. La esposa de mi hermano es mi* **(4)** ________________*, y los hijos de ellos son mis* **(5)** ________________*; mi madre es* **(6)** ________________ *de los hijos de mi hermano y* **(7)** ________________ *de la esposa de él.*

C Answer the following questions.

1 What is the maiden name of Pedro García's wife? ________________

2 What is her first name (*su nombre de pila*)? ________________

3 What is the first last name (*el primer apellido*) of her children?

____

4 What is their second last name (*el segundo apellido*)? ________________

5 Do the last names (*los apellidos*) of all the children in the chart follow this pattern? ____________

6 What would your *apellidos* be according to the Spanish naming system?

____

La celebración del matrimonio

Declaración de consentimiento

Elena, ¿quieres tomar a este hombre como tu esposo, para vivir juntos en el pacto del matrimonio; para amarlo, confortarlo, honrarlo y cuidarlo, tanto en tiempo de enfermedad como de salud; y, renunciando a todos los demás, quieres serle fiel mientras los dos vivan?

«Sí, quiero».

Ricardo, ¿quieres tomar a esta mujer como tu esposa, para vivir juntos en el pacto del matrimonio; para amarla, confortarla, honrarla y cuidarla, tanto en tiempo de enfermedad como de salud; y, renunciando a todas las demás, quieres serle fiel mientras los dos vivan?

«Sí, quiero».

Ustedes, testigos de este consentimiento, ¿harán cuanto puedan para sostener a estas dos personas en su matrimonio?

«Sí, lo haremos».

Matrimonio

En el nombre de Dios, yo, **Ricardo**, te recibo a ti, **Elena**, para ser mi esposa, desde hoy en adelante, para tenerte y conservarte, en las alegrías y las penas, en la riqueza y en la pobreza, en la salud y la enfermedad, para amarte y cuidarte hasta que la muerte nos separe. Este es mi voto solemne.

En el nombre de Dios, yo, **Elena**, te recibo a ti, **Ricardo**, para ser mi esposo, desde hoy en adelante, para tenerte y conservarte, en las alegrías y las penas, en la riqueza y en la pobreza, en la salud y la enfermedad, para amarte y cuidarte hasta que la muerte nos separe. Este es mi voto solemne.

Puesto que **Elena y Ricardo** se han dado el uno al otro por medio de votos solemnes, con la unión de las manos y con la entrega y recepción de anillos, yo los declaro esposo y esposa, en el Nombre del Padre, y del Hijo y del Espíritu Santo.

A quien Dios ha unido, nadie los separe.

EJERCICIOS

SCANNING FOR DETAILS

A Scan the selection to find the answers to the following questions.

1 Who is getting married? ______________________

2 Is this a religious or civil ceremony? ______________

3 Are the vows the same for the man as for the woman? __________

4 Do both the bride and groom receive rings? __________

USING WORD FORMATION TO DETERMINE MEANING

Spanish infinitives end in *-ar*, *-er*, or *-ir*. A feminine noun ending in *-ión* can often be derived from a verb.

declarar	to declare	*la declaración*	the declaration
unir	to unite	*la unión*	the union

B Using the same pattern, write in the missing forms below.

	VERB	NOUN
1	*concentrar*	________________
2	________________	*la celebración*
3	*renunciar*	________________
4	________________	*la conservación*
5	________________	*la separación*
6	*reunir*	________________

The present subjunctive, which changes the *-a* of an *-ar* verb to *-e*, and the *-e* of an *-er* or *-ir* verb to *-a,* can be used to indicate future actions that may or may not occur.

vivir	*mientras los dos* ***vivan***
to live	as long as they **live**

C Write the Spanish expression from the selection that corresponds to the future possibilities that appear in bold type below.

1 Will you do **what you can** . . . ? ______________________

2 . . . until death **separates us** ______________________

The suffix *-eza* transforms an adjective into a feminine noun that expresses the essence of the adjective.

gran	great/magnificent	*la grandeza*	magnificence
noble	noble	*la nobleza*	nobility
gentil	kind	*la gentileza*	kindness

D Write the Spanish equivalent of the following nouns as expressed in the selection, then write the corresponding adjective of each.

	NOUN	ADJECTIVE
1 wealth	________________	________________
2 poverty	________________	________________

USING CONTEXT TO DETERMINE MEANING

E Read the following sentences, then write the meaning of the words that appear in bold type.

1 *Promete renunciar a todos* ***los demás/las demás****.* ________________

2 *Ustedes son* ***testigos*** *de este consentimiento.* ________________

3 *¿Harán lo que puedan para* ***sostener*** *a estas dos personas en su matrimonio?*

____

4 *Te recibo para ser mi esposo* ***desde hoy en adelante****.*

____

UNDERSTANDING DISCOURSE MARKERS

Certain expressions indicate relationships between words and phrases.

tanto... como	as much . . . as
puesto que...	since/because

F Answer the following questions.

1 How is *tanto... como* used in the marriage ceremony?

____

2 What is the sentence in the selection that gives the celebrant the authority to declare the couple *"esposo y esposa"*?

____

____

____

____

A mi hija Flor de María

por Carlomagno Araya

En mi propia casa, desde el otro día
tengo una muñeca de carne y de hueso.
Aunque es un confite la muñeca mía,
¡yo no me la como sino que la beso!

¿Quién puso en sus labios fragante ambrosía,
quién en sus pupilas dejó el amor preso
y quién guardó para mi Flor de María
tan dulces encantos que dan embeleso?

Apenas un año cumplió y nos demanda
un lugar bien amplio, pues ya casi anda
y ha sido por eso, tan sólo por eso
que en mi alma he formado campo a su alegría.
Aunque es un confite mi Flor de María,
¡yo no me la como sino que la beso!

---

www.poesiasypoemas.com/ticos.

EJERCICIOS

SKIMMING FOR MEANING

A Read the poem quickly, then answer the following questions.

1 Who wrote the poem? ______________________________

2 Whom is the poem about? ______________________________

SCANNING FOR DETAILS

B Answer the following questions.

1 What is the child's name? ______________________________

2 How old is she? ______________________________

3 What is she almost able to do? ______________________________

4 What two things does the author compare her to?

____

5 How does he feel about her? ______________________________

COLOMBIA

La familia: un invento maravilloso

por Ligia Ochoa Sierra

Si me preguntas qué es la familia, te diré que es un lugar calientico, lleno de tranquilidad y de solidaridad. Por lo menos eso es mi familia. Cuando llego a casa me siento en otro mundo, es como cuando sales de un gran ruido y llegas a un lugar silencioso, con música muy suave y relajante. Y no es que en mi familia no haya problemas y una que otra angustia de vez en cuando, pero tienes la certeza de que las cosas se solucionan, de que todo va a pasar porque el lazo de amor es más fuerte que un inconveniente, por muy grave que este sea.

La familia es como los amigos, contados con los dedos de la mano, siempre seguros y presentes cuando los necesitas. Cuando no estás cerca de ellos, los extrañas mucho, sientes que algo te falta, que las cosas ya no te sonríen.

No siempre pensé así acerca de la familia. Durante algún tiempo pensaba en ella como algo agobiante, con muchos deberes y pocos derechos. A mi madre la sentía como un general, dando órdenes, impartiendo disciplina, exigiendo buenos resultados, insistiendo en lo mucho que ha hecho por los hijos, en lo que es correcto e incorrecto; en fin, dictaminándolo todo. Sin embargo, siempre, incluso en los años de rebeldía, me gustaba retornar a casa, estarme allí, vivir la cotidianidad, saberme un miembro de mi familia, aunque no tenía mucha conciencia de ello.

Cuando me fui a estudiar al extranjero, empecé a echar de menos las ventajas del hogar, lo bueno que se vive en el "hotel mamá", como se suele decir. Añoraba una persona que me saludara al llegar, que me tuviera la comida caliente y las historias de la gran familia o de los vecinos. Y eso que yo nunca he sido de las que habla mucho con sus padres o hermanos, pero la sensación de sentirme totalmente sola me acompañaba diariamente. Y como cosa rara, empecé a hablar con mi familia con mucha frecuencia, a contarle a mi madre cosas que antes no le hubiera contado por ningún motivo.

Después, formé mi propio hogar y me propuse hacerlo un lugar agradable, como había sido el mío. Un sitio de compinches, de cómplices, de escuchas atentos. Un club de aplausos o mejor de voces de aliento para emprender tareas nuevas, para conquistar el mundo, para lograr que no te pisoteen, para superar las dificultades diarias y para sobrellevar o vencer los múltiples defectos que tenemos como humanos. Yo, por ejemplo, soy una persona muy tímida y encuentro en mi hogar el espacio para extrovertirme pero también para ser tímida sin tener que ocultarlo, sin avergonzarme por ello, sin sentir el miedo social que a veces me agobia.

Ahora soy madre y comprendo mucho más a mi mamá, aunque tenemos algunas diferencias. Seguramente, pronto mi hijo me verá como un general y se repetirá la historia, espero que un poco mejor. Este es el milagro de la familia, de los ciclos vitales, en fin, de la vida.

EJERCICIOS

SKIMMING FOR GENERAL MEANING

A Read the selection quickly, then answer the following questions.

1 Does the author believe the family to be important? ______________

2 Have her feelings changed over time? ______________

USING CONTEXT TO DETERMINE MEANING

B Read the following sentences, then write the meaning of the words that appear in bold type.

1 *Cuando no estás cerca de ellos, los* ***extrañas*** *mucho.* ____________________

2 *Soy muy tímida, pero en mi casa no tengo que sentir el miedo social que a veces me* ***agobia****.* ____________________

3 *Pensaba que la familia era* ***agobiante****, con muchos deberes y pocos derechos.*

____

4 *Cuando me fui a estudiar al extranjero, empecé a* ***echar de menos*** *las ventajas del hogar.* ____________________

5 *Cuando estaba lejos de mi país y no conocía a nadie,* ***añoraba*** *una persona que me saludara al llegar.* ____________________

APPRECIATING ARTISTIC LANGUAGE

C What images do the following expressions bring to mind? Can you relate to them personally?

1 *las cosas no te sonríen* ____________________

2 *a mi mamá la sentía como un general* ____________________

3 *el hotel mamá* ____________________

4 *un club de aplausos* ____________________

REREADING FOR GREATER UNDERSTANDING

D Read the selection again, then tell how the author defines "family" in terms of the past, the present, and the future.

1 Past ____________________

2 Present ____________________

3 Future ____________________

La familia de Marcela

por Ligia Ochoa Sierra

Marcela vive con su madre, hermana y sobrina. Es una familia pequeña y muy unida aunque suelen hablar poco de sus problemas íntimos. Eso no quiere decir que no se comuniquen entre sí, sino más bien es como una especie de comunicación en silencio. Pareciera como si cada una de ellas guardara cierto rincón para sí misma, con el fin de desempeñarse mejor como miembro de la familia. Ellas tienen la idea de que la armonía en la familia, y mucho más en el amor, sólo es posible cuando cada persona tiene su propio proyecto de vida, sus luchas, sus logros y sus pérdidas.

La madre de Marcela, Ana, se separó hace muchos años porque su esposo la traicionó y porque no quiso seguirla a la ciudad para que sus "niñas"—como ella las llama—pudieran estudiar y "ser alguien en la vida". Desde entonces, trabajó duro para mantener y educar a sus hijas y ahora ambas son profesionales.

Juliana, la hermana de Marcela, estudió estadística pues era un verdadero genio para las matemáticas y Marcela se dedicó a las letras. Debe ser por aquello de la complementariedad. Juliana se casó y tuvo una hermosa niña pero se volvió a repetir la historia y a los 5 años de casada se separó. El esposo era un buen hombre pero un poco bohemio y quizá sin muchas metas e ilusiones.

La sobrina de Marcela, Juanita, es una niña morena, con unos ojazos negros, unas cejas largas y abundantes y una mirada muy intensa. Es muy inteligente y sensible. La separación de sus padres la afectó mucho y, como no es muy expresiva, fue muy difícil ayudarla.

Marcela es la soltera de la casa. Podría decirse mejor la solterona pues tiene casi 37 años y aún no se casa. Claro que no es la típica solterona triste y amargada. Está buscando un hombre con unas características muy especiales: bueno, inteligente, organizado con el dinero y a la vez generoso (Marcela odia los tacaños pero también a los que derrochan el dinero ya sea para presumir o por el deseo incontrolado de gastar). Ella no quiere equivocarse ni seguir el camino de

---

su madre y hermana pues piensa, como las abuelas antiguas, que el matrimonio es para toda la vida. Ha tenido varios pretendientes pero ninguno reúne todas las condiciones y eso que esas condiciones no son tan exigentes, pero parece que los hombres son muy imperfectos, seguramente porque les falta media costilla, —¡Quién lo sabe!

EJERCICIOS

UNDERSTANDING RELATIONSHIPS BETWEEN PHRASES

A Certain words in Spanish show how two or more phrases or clauses relate to each other. The following English sentences are translated from the selection; write the Spanish expression that corresponds to the English words that appear in bold type.

1 This doesn**'t** mean they don't communicate, **but** is **rather** a kind of silent communication. ____________ ____________

2 Harmony within a family, and **even more** in love, is only possible when each person has his own goals in life. ____________

3 He refused to follow her to the city **just so** her little girls could study.

____

4 Juliana studied statistics **because as a matter of fact** she was a true genius at math. ____________

5 It must be **attributed to** balance. ____________

6 You could probably say "old maid" **because as a matter of fact** she's almost 37. ____________

7 She is **certainly** not your typical sad and embittered old maid.

____

8 Marcela doesn't like stingy guys or those who throw away their money, **whether it be** to impress or because of the uncontrollable need to spend.

____

9 She doesn't want to follow in her mother's and sister's footsteps, **for** she feels, like the women in past generations, that marriage is for life.

____

USING A SPANISH-SPANISH DICTIONARY TO DETERMINE MEANING

B Many Spanish words do not have cognates in English; however, words in their dictionary definitions very often do. Look up the following words and phrases in a Spanish-Spanish dictionary, and see how the definitions not only help you determine the meaning of the word you have looked up, but also help to improve your vocabulary. Then look at the words in the context of the Spanish sentences below and write their English meaning.

1 ***soler (ue)*** + *infinitivo* • *hacer por hábito/hacer con frecuencia*

Es una familia muy unida aunque ***suelen*** *hablar poco.*

____

2 ***lograr*** • *obtener*
logro • *obtención*
ANTÓNIMOS
perder • *dejar de tener, por desgracia*
pérdida • *lo que ya no tiene*

Cada persona tiene sus propios ***logros*** *y* ***pérdidas****.*

________________________ ________________________

3 ***volver a*** + *infinitivo* • *hacer una vez más/empezar de nuevo*

Se ***volvió a*** *repetir la historia.* ________________________

4 ***a la vez*** • *al mismo tiempo/también*

Busca un hombre organizado con el dinero y ***a la vez*** *generoso.*

____

5 ***pretender*** • *intentar conquistar*
pretendiente • *uno que intenta conquistar*

Ha tenido varios ***pretendientes*** *pero ninguno reúne todas las condiciones.*

____

6 ***costilla*** • *uno de los huesos largos y arqueados que nacen de la columna vertebral y que forman la caja torácica*

Los hombres son imperfectos, seguramente porque les falta ***media costilla****.*

____

RECOGNIZING FALSE COGNATES

Occasionally a Spanish word fools us: it looks like an English word, but it has a different meaning. Some people call these *"amigos falsos."* Following are Spanish words with their true English meaning.

sensato	sensible
sensible	sensitive

C Complete the following sentence.

Juanita es una niña ______________ *pero* ______________.
(sensible) (sensitive)

REREADING FOR GREATER UNDERSTANDING

D Read the selection again. Does the last line make you laugh, smile, or feel annoyed, or in any way change your opinion of Marcela?

____

Un padre

La relación del maestro Fernando Botero con sus hijos es muy especial.

Lina y Fernando empiezan a recordar los momentos de la infancia, cuando pasaban las vacaciones junto a su padre en Nueva York. «Mi papá no tenía dinero», comenta Fernando, «pero nunca le faltó la creatividad. Una Navidad le pedimos un tren eléctrico, pero como no tenía con qué comprarlo, recogió latas de la basura, las llevó a su estudio y nos hizo unas armaduras y unas espadas; fueron los mejores regalos». «Pero la mejor anécdota», explica Lina muerta de la risa, «es la de la sopa de ojos: una vez, mi papá fue a una tienda de prótesis que había en la esquina de su casa y compró tres pares de ojos de cristal para usarlos en sus esculturas. En la noche preparó una sopa de cenar y nos dijo que era un platillo que nos iba a ayudar a ver mejor. Sin que nos diéramos cuenta, ¡le echó los ojos! Mientras tomábamos la sopa, éstos nos miraban constantemente... Él jamás soltó ni siquiera una sonrisa que nos pudiera hacer pensar que se trataba de una broma; fue una cena aterradora».

Adaptada de "Fernando Botero en Zihuantanejo", *Quién*, 1 de junio de 2001, p. 87.

EJERCICIOS

USING WORD FORMATION TO DETERMINE MEANING

In a narrative, the imperfect tense is used to describe action in the background, including activities that were already in progress when other events occurred. Imperfect forms end in *-aba* or *-ía* (with person and number endings). There are two exceptions.

ir	*iba*	*íbamos*	***ser***	*era*	*éramos*
	ibas			*eras*	
	iba	*iban*		*era*	*eran*

A Write the Spanish equivalent of the following expressions.

1 My father didn't have much money

____

2 There was a store on the corner near his house

____

3 the soup was a dish that was going to help us see better

____

4 While we were eating the soup

____

5 the eyes looked at us constantly

____

6 it was a joke

____

In a narrative, the preterite tense is used to relate the events that tell the story. Preterite forms for the third-person singular end in *-ó/-ió/-o*, with one exception: *ir* uses the form *fue*.

B In the selection, find the Spanish equivalent of the following sentences and clauses and write them in the space provided.

1 One Christmas we asked him for an electric train.

____

2 He got tin cans from the trash,

____

3 took them to his studio,

____

4 and made us armor and swords.

____

5 Dad went to a prosthesis shop

____

6 and bought three pairs of glass eyes.

____

7 He made soup for dinner and told us . . .

____

8 He put the eyes in it

____

9 He never cracked a smile

____

10 It was a scary meal.

____

READING FOR COMPREHENSION

C Read the entire selection again, then answer the following questions.

1 *¿Cómo era este padre?*

____

2 *¿Dónde vivía?*

____

3 *¿Cuándo lo visitaban sus hijos?*

____

4 *¿Qué querían los niños para la Navidad?*

____

5 *¿Qué les regaló el padre?*

____

6 *¿Fueron buenos regalos?*

____

7 *En otra ocasión, ¿qué puso en la sopa?*

____

8 *¿Estas son buenas o malas memorias?*

____

Los abuelos

Tarea para los alumnos del 4º grado:

En esta actividad, tienes que ir con tus abuelos y preguntarles sobre su vida cuando eran niños. Pregúntales sobre sus juegos, diles que te los enseñen. Luego, tú enséñales los juegos de ahora. Te aseguramos que se van a divertir a lo grande.

—y los niños respondieron:

Yo soy Miguel. Mis abuelos jugaban al avión, al trompo, escondidas, canicas, encantados y muñecas de trapo. Yo juego a huye, básquetbol, fútbol, nintendo 64, escondidas, carreras y otros. Opino que los juegos de ahora son diferentes que los de hace tiempo. Me gustan más los de ahora.

Hola me llamo Marcos y les voy a contar lo que jugaban mis abuelos cuando eran pequeños. A las escondidillas. Las escondidillas se juegan así: primero eligen a uno para que cuente mientras que los otros niños que juegan se esconden y cuando termina el niño que cuenta, sale a buscar y al primero que encuentre ése hace cuenta.

Soy Laurita. Les voy a contar a qué jugaban mis abuelitos. Jugaban al avión, las escondidas, la gallinita ciega, trompo, doña Blanca, Emiliano, adivinanzas y a la cuerda. Ahora yo juego Barbis, básquetbol, también juego a la gallina ciega, nintendo, computadora, a patinar y a carrerita.

Hola soy Alex. Tengo nueve años. Gracias a este proyecto les puedo contar que mis abuelitos jugaban al trompo de madera con punta de clavo, también jugaban balero y mi abuelita jugaba a las muñecas de trapo.

Hola me llamo Nayeli, tengo 9 años. Mi abuelita es muy dulce conmigo. Mi abuelita jugaba a muñeca de trapo y trastecitos de barro y mi abuelito trompo de madera y canicas de barro.

Yo me llamo Luisa Elena. Les voy a contar a lo que jugaban mis abuelos: Mi abuelita jugaba al columpio, a la cuerda, a la víbora de la mar, Doña Blanca, al burro pateado. Mi abuelito jugaba al palillo, al guajimare que es una bola de madera que se tira con el pie, a la cuarta escondida, al burro y a la escondidilla.

Yo estuve con mi abuelito y le pregunté —oye abue ¿tú jugabas a la Rueda de San Miguel? —y me contestó: «Sí, ese juego no me agradaba, era muy aburrido, solamente lo jugué como tres veces porque yo era un niño muy travieso».

Mis abuelitos jugaban a la rueda de San Miguel. Se juega así: todos forman una rueda y cantan.

Mi abuela jugaba a los listones, ollitas y rueda de San Miguel. Ella hacía muchas travesuras como cualquier joven.

Soy Tamara. Mi abuela se llama Marta. Ella jugaba a la matatena y se juega así: se ponen unas cruces en el piso y con una pelota las agarran.

Mi abuela me dijo: Por supuesto jugábamos a la Rueda de San Miguel, la cantábamos y uno por uno se iba volteando hasta que todos quedábamos al revés. Soy Paulina.

EJERCICIOS

SKIMMING FOR THE GENERAL IDEA

A Read the entire selection quickly, then answer the following questions.

1 For whom is this project intended? ______________________

2 What are they supposed to do?

____

____

USING CONTEXT TO DETERMINE MEANING

B Find the following Spanish words in the selection (some may appear more than once). After reading them in context, match them with their English equivalent(s).

1	_____, _____ *contar (ue)*	a	to find
2	_____, _____ *cuerda*	b	string
3	_____ *encontrar (ue)*	c	to tell
4	_____ *mientras*	d	rag
5	_____ *barro*	e	to count
6	_____ *trapo*	f	while
		g	rope
		h	clay

USING A SPANISH-SPANISH DICTIONARY TO DETERMINE MEANING

Because dictionary definitions often have recognizable cognates, they can be very helpful in determining the meaning of a word.

adivinar · *conocer algo por intuición*
adivinanza · *juego, en el cual se adivinan las respuestas*
agarrar · *tomar con la mano*
olla · *vasija redonda que sirve para cocer*
pelota · *juguete esférico, de material blando*
trastos · *utensilios que se emplean en alguna actividad*
travesura · *actividad de niños, que puede molestar o ser peligrosa*
travieso/a · *inquieto, bullicioso, que comete travesuras*

C Using the words in bold type above, complete the following sentences.

1 *Para jugar al fútbol, se necesita una* ________________.
2 *Ese niño es muy travieso, comete muchas* ________________.
3 *En la cocina, se necesitan* ________________ *y* ________________.
4 *Un buen juego para hacer en el coche con los niños es la* ________________.
5 *Para jugar a la cuerda, dos niñas tienen que* ________________ *la cuerda.*
6 *Una "ollita" es una pequeña* ________________.
7 *Un "trastecito" es un pequeño* ________________.

USING NEW WORDS AS CONTEXT CLUES

D Read the following directions for games and write the English meaning of the words that appear in bold type. Then determine the identity of each game and write its English name.

1 ***Escondidillas/Escondidas***

Primero ***eligen*** *a uno para que* ***cuente*** *mientras que los otros niños que juegan* ***se esconden****. Cuando termina el niño que cuenta, sale a buscar. Al primero que encuentre, ése hace cuenta.*

________________ ________________ ________________

Name of the game in English ________________________

2 ***La Rueda de San Miguel***

Todos forman una ***rueda*** *y cantan.*

____

This game has no equivalent in English-speaking countries.

3 ***La matatena***

*Se ponen unas **cruces** en el piso y con una pelota pequeña las **agarran**.*

__________________ __________________

Name of the game in English ____________________________

4 ***La cuerda***

*Dos niñas agarran la **cuerda** y le dan vueltas, mientras otra niña salta.*

____

Name of the game in English ____________________________

5 ***El trompo***

*El **trompo** es un juguete hecho de madera, tiene forma de cono con punta. La parte de arriba es redonda. Con una cuerda, el niño hace bailar al trompo.*

____

Name of the game in English ____________________________

REREADING FOR COMPREHENSION

E Read the entire selection again, then answer the following questions.

1 *¿Qué hacen los niños en este proyecto?*

____

2 *¿Qué hacían los abuelos cuando eran niños?*

____

____

3 *¿Qué actividades hacen los niños hoy?*

____

4 *En tu opinión, ¿qué juegos son más divertidos, los de los abuelos o los de ahora?* ____

5 *¿Crees que este proyecto fue una buena tarea para los niños? ¿Por qué sí o por qué no?* ____

Cuentos

por Renato Prada Oropeza

Nº 8

Hoy tengo que cenar con Maribel, mi ex-esposa. Lo hacemos cada año, puntualmente, desde el día que nos separamos, para celebrar ese acontecimiento. Cada uno habla durante treinta minutos, sin interrupción alguna. Cuenta todo lo bueno que le ha pasado en el transcurso del año: lo bueno real o imaginario, eso carece de importancia. En efecto, no tenemos que inventar mucho para hacer que el rubor de rabia y celos empiece a aflorar en la cara del otro. Después comemos y bebemos en silencio. Terminada la cena, nos separamos con un nudo amargo en la garganta que tardará un año en disolverse.

Nº 10

Hoy ha vuelto papá después de veinte años de ausencia. Nos sorprendió con su decisión de llevarnos a todos al lugar de donde vino. Estamos reunidos, considerando precisamente los detalles del viaje... Todos, excepto la abuela que, tercamente, se aferra a sus remedios caseros para prolongar su ya tan larga agonía.

Renato Prada Oropeza, *A través del hueco,* 1998.

EJERCICIOS

USING WORD PATTERNS TO DETERMINE MEANING

The word *lo* can refer to a previously mentioned activity.

Mi papá ***va a llevarme a un restaurante. Lo*** *hace siempre el día de mi cumpleaños.*	My father **is taking me to a restaurant**. He always does **that** on my birthday.

Lo que means "what" in the sense of "that which."

Lo que *vamos a hacer es un secreto.*	**What** we're going to do is a secret.
No me gusta ***lo que*** *dicen.*	I don't like **what** they say.

The construction *lo* + masculine singular adjective expresses the essence of the adjective as an abstract noun.

lo triste	the sad thing or things/what is sad
lo sorprendente	the surprising thing or things/what is surprising

A Answer the following questions.

1 What does *lo* refer to in the following sentence from the selection?

Lo hacemos cada año. ________________________________

2 How does the author express the following ideas?

a all the good things ________________________________

b the good things, whether real or imaginary

____

USING CONTEXT TO DETERMINE MEANING

B Read the following sentences, then write the meaning of the words that appear in bold type.

1 *Lo hacemos cada año, desde el día que nos separamos, para celebrar ese* ***acontecimiento****.* ________________

2 *Cuenta lo bueno que le ha pasado en el* ***transcurso*** *del año.*

____

3 *Si es real o imaginario* ***carece de*** *importancia.* ________________

4 *El* ***rubor*** *de rabia y celos empieza a* ***aflorar*** *en la cara.*

________________ ________________

5 *Nos separamos con un* ***nudo*** *amargo en la garganta.* ________________

READING FOR COMPREHENSION

C Read each story carefully, then answer the following questions.

In story Nº 8:

1 Whom is the author going to see? ____________________

2 What are they celebrating? ____________________

3 How often do they do this? ____________________

4 What is their conversation like? ____________________

5 Do they argue? __________

6 How long does it take each one to recover? ____________________

In story Nº 10:

7 Who came back today? ____________________

8 How long had he been away? ____________________

9 Where is he taking everybody? ____________________

10 Who isn't going? ____________________

11 Why is she suffering? ____________________

El estilo de vida hoy

Entérate
Actualidad
Chicas Terra
Deportes
Derecho y Negocios
Economía
Educación
Entretenimiento
Gente Terra
Mujer y Familia
Turismo
Tecnología
The Boy
Teodoro
Ver Más...

Diviértete
Oscar 2002
Cristian Castro
Alexandre Pires
Mundial 2002
Ver Más...

Participa
Chat
Intermedia
Foros
Instanterra
Humor
Ver Más...

Servicios
Páginas Amarillas
Buscador LYCOS
Empleos
Mall de Compras
Disco Virtual
Horóscopo
Horóscopo Semanal
Loterías
Tarot
Tienda Terra 
W. Mercado
Diccionario
Ver Más...

Terra Venezuela

www.terra.com.ve.

EJERCICIO

SCANNING FOR INFORMATION

A Look carefully at the web page, then answer the following questions.

1 What is the date of this page? ______________________

2 What holiday is coming up? ______________________

3 What is the name of the highway that is being closed during the holidays?

____

4 What two things can you register your opinion on?

____

5 Where would you *"hacer clic"* if you were looking for a job?

____

6 What can you get three of for the price of two? ______________________

7 What is the name of Alexandre Pires's new single? ______________________

8 What can you find here for young children?

____

9 What is the name of a popular computer game in Spanish?

____

10 Where would you *"hacer clic"* for financial information?

____

11 Is there access to shopping through the Internet? If so, where would you *"hacer clic"*? ______________________

12 In what places could you look for "fortune-telling" advice?

____

13 What information do you have to enter in order to get e-mail through Terra?

____

14 How could you get in touch with Terra Networks?

____

Mi PC

por Juan Luis Guerra

Niña, te quiero decir
que tengo en computadora
un gigabyte de tus besos
y un floppy de tu persona.
Niña, te quiero decir
que sólo tú me interesas
y el mouse que mueve tu boca
me formatea la cabeza.

Niña, te quiero decir
que en mi PC sólo tengo
un monitor con tus ojos
y un CD-Rom de tu cuerpo.
Niña, te quiero decir
que el internet de mis sueños
lo conecté a tu sonrisa
y al modem de tus cabellos.
Y yo quiero mandarte un recadito
ábreme tu e-mail
y enviarte un diskette
con un poquito de mi
cariñito
bueno para amarte.

Coro
Yo no quiero un limousine,
ni un chaleco de Hugo Boss,
ni la Cindy Crawford en Berlín,
ni un palacio con pagodas quiero yo.

Yo no quiero Burger King,
ni un dibujo de Miró.
Morenita, no me hagas sufrir.
Tu cariño por la noche quiero yo.

EJERCICIO

SCANNING FOR DETAILS

A Read the *letra* to this song carefully, then answer the following questions.

1 To whom is the song addressed? ______

2 Where does the singer keep his memories? ______

3 What does he have a gigabyte of? ______

4 What does he have on a floppy disk? ______

5 What moves her mouth? ______

6 What formats his mind? ______

7 What feature does his monitor have? ______

8 What does he have a CD-ROM of? ______

9 What did he connect his imaginary internet to? ______

10 What attachment does he want to send with his e-mail message?

______

11 What six things does the singer not care about?

______ ______

______ ______

______ ______

12 What does he want, and when? ______

Cristina

Esta es la primera vez, desde que comencé *Cristina*, que me dedico a organizar mis pensamientos en papel acerca de todo lo que me ha sucedido en la vida hasta el momento actual. Es un proceso de reflexión y análisis, pero también de orientación. Y lo que quiero comunicarles a ustedes—sobre todo a los jóvenes—es el poder formidable de la voluntad, y las repercusiones a largo plazo de las decisiones y las acciones que tomamos en la vida.

Siempre se nos dice que "Querer es poder", pero nadie nos explica cómo y de qué forma es posible *querer* hasta *poder*. Nadie nos cuenta cómo se hizo rico, cómo llegó a ser famoso, o cómo alcanzó un grado relativo de felicidad en la vida. Yo quiero contarles cómo yo lo hice. Y si alguien quiere seguir el camino que ya yo he andado, ¡aquí está!

No solamente está lleno de gloria y de fama, de riquezas y de situaciones bellas.

Está lleno de baches, de espinas y a veces, hasta de lodo.

¡Está lleno de temores!

Está lleno de... todo.

Pero eso es la vida.

Prepárate para aprender y para cambiar. Y prepárate bien, porque no es fácil lograr las metas que nos trazamos en la vida. ¡Para nadie!

Pero sí te garantizo que vale la pena, tomando en consideración las alternativas. Y lo digo porque yo tuve que *aprender* y *cambiar*... y hoy quiero comunicarles mis experiencias con toda la comprensión y el amor del mundo.

Cristina Saralegui, *¡Cristina! Confidencias de una rubia*, p. 5.

EJERCICIOS

USING COGNATES TO DETERMINE MEANING

A Scan the selection to find the Spanish equivalent of the following words, then write them in the space provided.

Nouns

1	moment	____________	9	glory	____________
2	process	____________	10	fame	____________
3	reflection	____________	11	situation	____________
4	analysis	____________	12	consideration	____________
5	orientation	____________	13	alternative	____________
6	repercussion	____________	14	experience	____________
7	decision	____________	15	comprehension	____________
8	action	____________			

Adjectives

1	formidable	____________	3	famous	____________
2	possible	____________	4	relative	____________

Verbs

1	organize	____________	3	prepare	____________
2	communicate	____________	4	guarantee	____________

B Find the nouns in Exercise A that end in *-ión.*

1 What gender are they? ____________

Using the *-ión* pattern, write the noun forms of the first three verbs in Exercise A.

2 ____________

3 ____________

4 ____________

RECOGNIZING FALSE COGNATES

Following are Spanish words with their true English meaning.

verdadero	actual
actual	current/present
corriente	ordinary

C Complete the following sentences.

1 *Esta no es una revista* ____________ (ordinary).

2 *Esta no es mi* ____________ (current) *dirección.*

3 *Esta no es mi* ____________ (actual) *dirección.*

The type of object pronoun used with a verb can change its meaning.

Dedicar, when used with an indirect object pronoun, means "to dedicate something to somebody."

Le *dedica el libro* ***a*** *su madre.*	He dedicates the book to his mother.

Dedicarse, a reflexive verb (which must always be used with a reflexive pronoun), means "to spend a lot of time doing/to devote oneself to."

Se *dedica a limpiar la casa.*	She spends a lot of time cleaning the house.
Se *dedica a su familia.*	She devotes herself to her family.

D Complete the following sentences.

1 *El profesor* ____dedica____ (spends a lot of time) *a leer todos los trabajos de sus estudiantes.*

2 *El profesor* ____dedica____ (dedicates) *su novela a su esposa.*

USING WORD FORMATION TO DETERMINE MEANING

The preterite tense, which is used to relate actions that began and ended in the past, uses two patterns for the first-person singular form. Most verbs follow pattern 1.

-ar verbs	infinitive form minus *-ar* + *é*
-er/-ir verbs	infinitive form minus *-er/-ir* + *í*

hablar	to speak	*habl* + *é* → *hablé*	I spoke
comer	to eat	*com* + *í* → *comí*	I ate
escribir	to write	*escrib* + *í* → *escribí*	I wrote

E Write the first-person singular preterite form for the following verbs.

1	*cambiar*	to change	I changed	____________
2	*contar*	to tell	I told	____________
3	*lograr*	to achieve	I achieved	____________
4	*preparar*	to prepare	I prepared	____________
5	*tomar*	to take	I took	____________

If the infinitive ends in *-car*, the first-person preterite ends in *-qué*.

tocar	to touch	*toqué*	I touched

If the infinitive ends in *-gar*, the first-person preterite ends in *-gué*.

jugar	to play	*jugué*	I played

If the infinitive ends in *-zar*, the first-person preterite ends in *-cé*.

empezar	to start	*empecé*	I started

F Write the first-person singular preterite form for the following verbs.

1	*comenzar*	to begin	I began	________________
2	*explicar*	to explain	I explained	________________
3	*llegar*	to arrive	I arrived	________________
4	*garantizar*	to guarantee	I guaranteed	________________
5	*organizar*	to organize	I organized	________________
6	*comunicar*	to communicate	I communicated	________________
7	*alcanzar*	to reach	I reached	________________
8	*dedicarse*	to spend time	I spent time	me ________________
9	*trazarse (metas)*	to set up (goals)	I set up (goals)	me ________________ (metas)

Many frequently used verbs follow pattern 2 to form the first-person singular preterite.

querer	to want	*quis* + e →	*quise*	I wanted
tener	to have	*tuv* + e →	*tuve*	I had
andar	to walk/go	*anduv* + e →	*anduve*	I walked/went
estar	to be	*estuv* + e →	*estuve*	I was
poder	to be able to	*pud* + e →	*pude*	I was able to
hacer	to do	*hic* + e →	*hice*	I did
decir	to say	*dij* + e →	*dije*	I said

G Complete the following sentences.

1 *Yo quiero contarle cómo lo* ________________ (I did).

2 *Y lo digo porque yo* ________________ que (I had to) *aprender y cambiar.*

FINDING COGNATES IN A SPANISH-SPANISH DICTIONARY

H Many of the words in bold type below do not have common cognates in English. However, the definition in a Spanish-Spanish dictionary (column 2) can lead you to the true meaning. Write the English meaning of the words and phrases that appear in bold type.

1	***a largo plazo***	*al final*	________________
2	***la voluntad***	*la intención firme*	________________
3	***la felicidad***	*la satisfacción*	________________
4	***el bache***	*una desigualdad en la calle/ momentos difíciles*	________________
5	***el lodo***	*la mezcla de tierra y agua*	________________
6	***el temor***	*la aprensión fuerte*	________________
7	***la meta***	*el objetivo*	________________
8	***valer la pena***	*servir para producir buenos resultados*	________________

READING FOR COMPREHENSION

I Read the selection again, then answer the following questions.

1 Has Cristina written an autobiography before? ____________

2 What does she consider to be extremely powerful? ________________

3 To whom is she speaking especially? ________________

4 What are some of the benefits of success?

____

5 What are some of the hardships on the road to success?

____

6 Is this easy for anyone? ____________

7 Is it worthwhile? ____________

8 What did Cristina have to do? ________________________

9 What does Cristina offer to her readers?

____

Oscar de la Renta

Oscar de la Renta, galardonado con el premio, "Diseñador del Año" del CFDA, dejó su país de nacimiento, la República Dominicana, a la edad de dieciocho años, para estudiar pintura en la Academia de San Fernando en Madrid.

Mientras vivía en España, descubrió su talento para la moda y empezó como dibujante en las casas de moda españolas, y rápidamente llegó a trabajar como aprendiz del costurero más cotizado de España, Cristóbal Balenciaga. Después de unos años, dejó España para juntarse con Antonio Castillo como ayudante en la casa de Lanvin en París. En 1963, vino a Nueva York para diseñar las colecciones de costura del salón Elizabeth Arden. En 1965 empezó su propia marca de *prêt à porter*, "Signature".

Durante treinta años, esta marca ha crecido y ahora incluye una colección refinada de ropa y accesorios basada en su propio estilo "Signature": su línea de ropa de deporte para hombres, OSCAR, una colección de Jeans para hombres y mujeres, OSCAR JEANS, y una colección contemporánea para las mujeres, O de Oscar de la Renta.

Sus perfumes—Oscar, Volupté y SO de la Renta para mujeres y Pour Lui y Oscar for Men para hombres—han logrado reconocimiento internacional.

Oscar de la Renta ha ganado premios en los Estados Unidos, España, Francia y la República Dominicana. Con su Colección de Primavera 1993 de Pierre Balmain llegó a ser el primer americano que diseñaba para una casa costurera francesa. Se reconoce, además, como filántropo: ha construido dos escuelas en la República Dominicana, adonde asisten unos 1.500 niños.

EJERCICIOS

USING WORD FORMATION TO DETERMINE MEANING

The suffixes *-nte/-dor/-ero* indicate the performer of an action or a person's occupation or position.

-nte	*amante*	lover
	cantante	singer
	representante	representative
-dor	*contador*	accountant
	profesor	teacher
	cazador	hunter
-ero	*barbero*	barber
	plomero	plumber
	cocinero	cook

A Find the words in the selection that follow these patterns, and write each word below, along with its meaning in English.

	SPANISH NOUN	ENGLISH MEANING
1 *-nte*	____________________	____________________
2 *-dor*	____________________	____________________
3 *-ero*	____________________	____________________

The suffix *-miento* changes a verb into a noun that signifies the action of the verb.

sufrir	to suffer	*el sufrimiento*	suffering
entrenar	to train	*el entrenamiento*	training
entretener	to entertain	*el entretenimiento*	entertainment
descubrir	to discover	*el descubrimiento*	discovery

B Following this pattern, write the noun form of each of the following verbs, along with its meaning in English.

	SPANISH NOUN	ENGLISH MEANING
1 *nacer*	____________________	____________________
2 *sentir*	____________________	____________________
3 *conocer*	____________________	____________________
4 *reconocer*	____________________	____________________

USING CONTEXT TO DETERMINE MEANING

C Read the following sentences, then write the meaning of the words that appear in bold type.

1 *Oscar ganó el* ***premio*** *"Diseñador del Año" del CFDA.* ____________

2 ***Dejó*** *su país de nacimiento para estudiar en España.* ____________

3 *Cristóbal Balenciaga era uno de los costureros más* ***cotizados*** *de España.*

____

4 *Vino a Nueva York para diseñar las colecciones de* ***costura*** *del salón Elizabeth Arden.* ____________

5 *En 1965 empezó su propia* ***marca****, "Signature".* ____________

6 *Durante treinta años, esta marca* ***ha crecido*** *y ahora incluye una colección de ropa y accesorios.* ____________

READING FOR COMPREHENSION

D Read the entire selection again, then answer the following questions.

1 Where is Oscar de la Renta from? ____________

2 What does he do? ____________

3 Where did he get his training?

____

4 What design houses has he worked for?

____________ ____________

____________ ____________

5 What is the name of his label? ____________

6 What are the names of his fragrances for men?

____________ ____________

7 What special project does he have in his native country?

____

Carolina Herrera, qué mujer

Hay algo en esta mujer—de una personalidad extraordinaria—que no deja lugar a dudas. Ha triunfado porque no había posibilidad de que esto no ocurriera. Como diseñadora ha sabido interpretar perfectamente los gustos y las necesidades de una mujer amante del lujo y la elegancia, alejándola de los excesos y las estridencias de otras líneas. Como empresaria ha sabido construir lenta e inexorablemente una firma que ya es todo un imperio. En 1980 presentó su primera colección de moda, en 1986, la primera de novias. En 1988 salía a la calle su primer perfume; en los próximos meses, lanza el sexto, 212 para hombre. En 1997 lanza su primera colección de accesorios y su primera línea de maquillaje. Y aparentemente... sin inmutarse.

Las proporciones de la moda la han convertido en una industria. ¿Afecta a un creador todo el marketing, el aparataje que rodea al diseñador?

CAROLINA HERRERA No puede afectar porque el proceso creador es el origen de todo. Sin la creación primera no hay nada. Lo que tú quieres hacer, lo que tú quieres ver en la mujer... nada de eso depende del proceso posterior. Una vez que se han traspasado las puertas del taller original, cuando ya hay producción de líneas, y ya no es producción individual, se necesita un aparataje de producción, ventas, distribución... así ha sido siempre. Pero no ha cambiado el origen, el momento de creación personal del diseñador, la decisión individual. Sin ese primer momento creativo, no hay nada.

Usted ha triunfado rotundamente en el mundo de la moda americana y latina. ¿Ha decidido hacerlo en Europa?

CH En Europa están todos mis perfumes. Pienso que algún día estará mi moda... pero no me lo planteo como algo que vaya a ocurrir en el futuro más inmediato. Todos los diseñadores europeos quieren conquistar América, Nueva York. Es interesante observar lo que está pasando ahora, porque Nueva York está en un momento impresionante. París es la capital de la moda y lo será siempre, pero ahora

---

Inés Aizpún, www.ENEL.net/Editorial AA.

Nueva York es una capital de la moda, y eso es algo que hace unos años ni siquiera se podía prever. ¿Ir a Europa? ¡Ahora los europeos quieren venir a América! Creo que estoy en el lugar adecuado, en el momento adecuado. La moda americana ha influido muchísimo en los europeos... sobre todo en esa faceta de ropa más deportiva. Creo que en realidad es la visión americana de la vida la que está influyendo en Europa de una manera global. Yo me considero una diseñadora americana porque todo lo que he hecho como diseñadora ha sido aquí, aunque nadie puede olvidar sus raíces, en mi caso, latinas.

Parecería que para una mujer diseñadora es más accesible el triunfo en América que en Europa...

CH Creo que no, que siempre ha habido mujeres, couturières, diseñadoras buenísimas y a las que se les ha reconocido el triunfo. Quizá las grandes firmas tienen hombres... pero ¿y Coco Chanel, por ejemplo? desde la época de María Antonieta ha habido en Francia grandes modistas. En España en concreto, hay más que en el resto de Europa.

¿La moda es cíclica, ¿qué nos toca llevar ahora?

CH La moda deberá cambiar cada tres meses...

Eso, sin duda, convendría a los diseñadores, pero no sé si convendría a las mujeres...

CH Es que la moda es efímera, esa es su propia esencia. El problema es que hoy en día la mujer quiere un uniforme, las mujeres no tienen la personalidad ni la necesidad de experimentar algo nuevo. Antes había mujeres con estilo propio, mujeres que seguían la moda muy a su manera, porque su propia personalidad interpretaba las propuestas. Tenían un sello, propio, no importa de qué nivel social hablemos o de qué poder adquisitivo. Los creadores, los diseñadores se inspiraban en las mujeres de la calle para averiguar qué necesitaban, qué querían, qué demandaba su forma de vivir. Hoy no puedes inspirarte en la calle porque todas las mujeres van vestidas de gris o de negro, o de lo que creen que hay que ir.

¿Qué propone, entonces?

CH La mujer tiene que ser más individual. Cada mujer tiene un cierto estilo, tiene que adaptarse a lo que le viene bien. Es un tópico pero es una gran verdad: hay que conocerse bien, no seguir ciegamente la moda.

A algunos diseñadores se les critica que sólo crean para mujeres muy jóvenes. Su moda es menos limitada...

CH ¡Mi ropa es superjoven! Mis hijas la llevan, sus amigas la llevan, son jóvenes y la llevan, todo depende de cómo lo llevas y cómo te veas. Hay una persona que lleva un vestido y le da su propia versión. Un vestido de matrona lo lleva una niña de 16 años y se ve joven.

¿En qué momento decide un diseñador crear su propio perfume? ¿Es una exigencia del marketing de marca o es un escalón en el proceso creativo?

CH Es lo más importante. Para un diseñador es fundamental tener un perfume. Es el ideal para todo diseñador, es tu nombre y tu personalidad, tu estilo y tu manera de entender la moda, es el producto que se vende por todo el mundo y hace tu nombre por encima de barreras y fronteras.

¿Qué papel juega el perfume en su concepto del estilo, de la moda?

CH Es crucial. Yo lo veo como el accesorio más importante de la mujer.

¿Cómo nace Carolina Herrera?

CH Era mi aroma. Yo lo mezclaba desde hacía años, para mí: aceite de jazmín y de nardos. Cuando vinieron de la compañía Puig para hacerlo profesionalmente, sabía muy claramente qué era lo que yo quería. Durante dos años trabajaron en él, me lo mandaban y yo lo probaba, opinaba. Dos años después nacía Carolina Herrera. Hasta que no llegó exactamente lo que yo quería no di mi aprobación.

Causan siempre gran impresión los vestidos de novia. ¿Cuándo comenzó esta línea?

CH Como línea propiamente de moda nupcial en el año 86, aunque siempre tenía una novia al acabar todos los desfiles. Ya no son tan tradicionales, siguen de blanco y quieren ser protagonistas del día más importante en la vida de una mujer. Quieren verse más jóvenes, y por eso hay vestidos cada vez más escotados, sin mangas. Si eres una novia tradicional de blanco tienes que ser más inocente. No la veo con mucho maquillaje.

EJERCICIOS

SKIMMING FOR GENERAL MEANING

A Read the entire selection quickly, then answer the following questions.

1 What does Carolina Herrera do? ______________________________

2 In what city has she established her business? ______________________

3 What three aspects of her work are mentioned here?

____

USING WORD FORMATION TO DETERMINE MEANING

The construction *haber* + participle is one way to express past action. The verb *haber* is conjugated as follows.

yo	*he*	*nosotros*	*hemos*
tú	*has*		
usted/él/ella	*ha*	*ustedes/ellos/ellas*	*han*

The participle is formed by adding *-ado* to the stem of *-ar* verbs, and *-ido* to the stem of *-er* and *-ir* verbs.

Some frequently used verbs have irregular participles.

abrir	*abierto*	*poner*	*puesto*
decir	*dicho*	*romper*	*roto*
escribir	*escrito*	*ver*	*visto*
hacer	*hecho*	*volver*	*vuelto*
morir	*muerto*		

B Find the verb forms in the selection that correspond to the following English expressions and write them in the space provided.

1 she succeeded (triumphed) ______________________

2 she knew ______________________

3 it has always been ______________________

4 it hasn't changed ______________________

5 have you decided . . . ? ______________________

6 it has influenced ______________________

7 I have done ______________________

8 there have always been ______________________

The suffix *-mente* often indicates an adverb that tells how something is done; this meaning is usually expressed in English by the suffix "-ly."

C Write the words from the selection that correspond to the following English words.

1 perfectly ______________________

2 slowly ______________________

3 surely (inexorably) ______________________

4 greatly (roundly) ______________________

5 blindly ______________________

6 professionally ______________________

7 clearly ______________________

8 exactly ______________________

USING A SPANISH-SPANISH DICTIONARY

The expressions in bold type below are commonly used in Spanish. You might find definitions in your Spanish-Spanish dictionary that are similar to the ones provided below.

todo un (imperio) · *un (imperio) que ya está hecho o completo*
todo diseñador · *todos los diseñadores*
ni siquiera · *enfáticamente, no*
sobre todo · *especialmente*
en concreto · *por ejemplo*
entonces · *en ese caso*
cada vez más · *más y más, gradualmente*

D Write the English meaning of the words that appear in bold type.

1 *Ha construido una firma que ya es* ***todo un imperio****.*

____

2 ***Todo diseñador*** *necesita crear su propio perfume.*

____

3 *La moda americana ha influido* ***sobre todo*** *en la ropa más deportiva.*

____

4 *En España,* ***en concreto****, hay más diseñadoras que en el resto de Europa.*

____

5 *Hay vestidos* ***cada vez más sencillos****.* ________________________

6 *Hace unos años* ***ni siquiera se podía imaginar*** *esto.*

____

7 *¿Qué propone,* ***entonces****?* ________________________

Following are several Spanish words and their definitions.

alejar · *distanciar*
lanzar · *introducir*
rodear · *estar o ir alrededor de algo o alguien*
plantearse · *considerar*
prever · *ver antes*
convenir · *ser bueno para una persona*
averiguar · *saber por primera vez*
al acabar · *al terminar, al final*

E Write the English meaning of the words that appear in bold type.

1 *Carolina Herrera sabe* ***alejar*** *a la mujer de los excesos de otras líneas.*

____

2 *En 1997* ***lanza*** *su primera colección de accesorios.* ________________________

3 *Muchas personas* ***rodean*** *a los diseñadores.* ________________

4 *"****No me lo planteo*** *como algo que vaya a ocurrir ahora".*

____

5 *No se puede* ***prever*** *el futuro.* ________________

6 *No* ***me conviene*** *comprar mucha ropa ahora.* ________________

7 *Los diseñadores observaban a las mujeres para* ***averiguar*** *qué necesitaban.*

____

8 *Carolina siempre tenía una novia* ***al acabar*** *todos los desfiles.*

____

REREADING FOR GREATER UNDERSTANDING

F Read the entire selection again, then answer the following questions.

1 What is special about Carolina Herrera's clothing lines?

____

2 Does she feel that marketing and other influences affect her designs?

____

3 How does she feel about New York?

____

4 Does she think it's easier for a female designer in the United States than in Europe? ________________

5 According to Carolina, how often should styles change? ________________

6 What does she expect women to do with her clothes?

____

7 Apart from clothing, what does she consider to be fundamental for every designer? ________________

8 How does she feel brides should look?

____

Edward James Olmos: Embajador de la buena voluntad

Detrás del reconocido actor y director de cine norteamericano hay un aura de sencillez y humildad que muy pocos artistas de su talla tendrán jamás. En su visita a El Salvador, recorrió varias comunidades indígenas con los representantes de UNICEF.

Con pantalón y camisa casual, y un gafete distintivo de UNICEF en su brazo izquierdo, Edward James Olmos visitó algunas comunidades indígenas de Sonsonate, en su esfuerzo por mejorar la calidad de vida de sus habitantes.

El actor dejó sus papeles y las cámaras de cine, para demostrar su interés por las personas más necesitadas, trabajo que ha venido desarrollando hace más de trece años como embajador voluntario de UNICEF. Olmos considera que los derechos de los niños son importantes porque "dan la autoestima que se necesita para ser, crecer y hacer todo en esta vida".

El embajador de buena voluntad señaló que en el mundo, los hombres se han acostumbrado a diferenciar las razas y a llamarlas "indígena, africana, anglosajona y latina" pero, "esas no son razas, son culturas... no más hay una raza, y esa es la humana", señaló.

Gracias a sus raíces latinas por parte de su madre, Olmos considera importante trabajar por la preservación de las comunidades indígenas, porque ahí se encuentra la verdadera identidad cultural.

En el recorrido fue acompañado por representantes de UNICEF. La primera comunidad a visitar fue el cantón San Ramón de San Antonio del Monte, llegando hasta la escuela Nahuat, un pequeño ranchito que los habitantes construyeron para dar clases de su propia lengua.

En ese lugar, Olmos escuchó por varios minutos las necesidades de estos jóvenes, que demandaron tener sus propios terrenos para el cultivo de sus plantas medicinales, seguir enseñando a sus descendientes el idioma nahuat e infundir sus propias costumbres. También

---

Alejandra Salcedo, *El diario de hoy*, www.elsalvador.com.

expusieron los problemas de salud y alimentación que enfrentan los niños de la zona, debido a sus escasos recursos económicos.

Entrega y humildad

El segundo sitio que visitó Olmos fue la colonia El Rosario del cantón Guacamaya en Nahuizalco, una comunidad afectada por la tormenta tropical Mitch. El lugar está rodeado de dos paredones de tierra y en medio unas casas improvisadas en las que viven 160 familias. Olmos también escuchó con atención las necesidades de los habitantes que, hasta con lágrimas en los ojos, narraban cómo el lodo había llevado sus casas y pertenencias. Una incertidumbre que va cobrando fuerza a medida que el invierno se acerca. Olmos aprovechó la oportunidad para demostrar a los habitantes su apoyo y tendía la mano a las personas reunidas, mientras a los pequeños les acariciaba su carita o los abrazaba.

El actor ha sido objeto de múltiples reconocimientos por su trabajo en el cine, la televisión y su humanismo, galardones que muchos artistas hubieran querido tener; sin embargo, Olmos asegura que no trabajó para ganar esos premios y su secreto fue siempre "hacer cada día, lo mejor que uno puede hacer" y tener la disciplina en el momento justo.

Compromisos y proyectos

Después, se dirigió a la radio Atunal, que en nahuat significa "Sol de río", una emisora indígena que presta servicio a su comunidad con escasos recursos técnicos. Ahí fue enterado sobre la historia de la radio y la manera en que operaban, luego fue entrevistado por Guillermo Tesorero, director de Atunal. Olmos contestó a las preguntas y por peticiones de los visitantes se tomó cuanta foto le pidieron; también aprovechó el momento para saludar a una anciana de 99 años de edad.

Una vez que había visto con sus propios ojos la necesidad de la gente, manifestó que regresaría con los datos y videos tomados para dar apoyo a UNICEF y los representantes se encargarían de distribuirlo. Aunque no dio fecha de su regreso, Olmos se mostró interesado en una nueva visita a El Salvador.

Entre los proyectos que le esperan están unos documentales para televisión y unas películas con temas latinoamericanos. "En los últimos 20 años hemos tenido más cosas de parte de la cultura latina, que en cualquier otra época del cine". Por el momento, está en el proyecto de una película que saldrá en dos años, porque les ha tardado cinco años en estudiar la historia. "Hemos leído más de 150 libros sobre los temas, les va a encantar porque nos van a entender como cultura latina".

Olmos terminó su visita en la Casa de la Cultura de Nahuizalco, con un aspecto cansado, pero muy satisfecho de su recorrido.

EJERCICIOS

SKIMMING FOR GENERAL MEANING

A Read the entire selection quickly, then answer the following questions.

1 Whom is this selection about? ______________________

2 Where is he from? ______________________

3 What is his usual type of work? ______________________

4 What did he visit, and where? ______________________

5 Why was he there? ______________________

6 Did he make a good impression? __________

SCANNING FOR DETAILS

B Read the selection carefully to find the answers to the following questions; write the answers below.

1 What kind of communities did Olmos visit in Sonsonate?

____

2 How long has he been a volunteer for UNICEF? ______________________

3 Why does he consider children's rights to be important?

____

4 How does he define the word *raza*?

____

5 Who was his Hispanic ancestor? ______________________

6 What is the *escuela Nahuat*? ______________________

7 What problems did they talk about in San Ramón de San Antonio del Monte?

____

____

8 What caused big problems for the village of *El Rosario*?

____

9 What does Olmos consider to be the secret to his success?

____

10 Where did he have his picture taken? ______________________________

11 What did he promise the people at the end of his visit?

____

____

12 What is the theme of his next movie? ______________________________

CHILE

Un día insólito

Entró en su oficina por la puerta de servicio, como hacía a menudo para evitar a los clientes de la sala de espera. Su escritorio era una montaña de papeles y en el suelo se apilaban también documentos y libros de consulta, sobre el sofá había un chaleco y varias cajas con campanitas y ciervos de cristal. El desorden crecía a su alrededor amenazando con devorarlo. Mientras se quitaba el impermeable pasó revista a las plantas, preocupado por el aspecto fúnebre de los helechos. No alcanzó a tocar el timbre, Tina lo esperaba con la agenda del día.

—Debemos hacer algo con esta calefacción, me está matando las plantas.

—Hoy tiene una declaración a las once y acuérdese que en la tarde debe ir a los tribunales. ¿Puedo acomodar un poco aquí? Esto parece un basural, si no le importa que se lo diga, Sr. Reeves.

—Bien, pero no me toque el archivo de Benedict, estoy trabajando en eso. Escriba otra vez al club de Navidad para que no me manden más chirimbolos. ¿Me puede traer una aspirina, por favor?

—Creo que le harán falta dos. Su hermana Judy ha llamado varias veces, es urgente —anunció Tina y salió.

Reeves tomó el teléfono y llamó a su hermana, quien le comunicó en pocas palabras que Shanon había pasado temprano a dejar a David en su casa antes de emprender viaje con rumbo desconocido.

—Ven a buscar a tu hijo cuanto antes porque no pienso hacerme cargo de este monstruo, bastante tengo con mis hijos y mi madre. ¿Sabes que ahora usa pañales?

—¿David?

—Mi mamá. Veo que tampoco sabes nada de tu propio hijo.

Isabel Allende, *El plan infinito*, pp. 283–84.

EJERCICIOS

SKIMMING FOR GENERAL MEANING

A Read the entire selection quickly, then answer the following questions.

1 What does the main character do? ______________________________

2 Where is he? ______________________________

3 With whom is his first conversation? ______________________________

4 What kind of state is he in? ______________________________

5 With whom is his second conversation? ______________________________

USING CONTEXT TO DETERMINE MEANING

B Read the following sentences, then write the meaning of the words that appear in bold type.

1 *Entró por la puerta de servicio para* ***evitar*** *a los clientes de la sala de espera.*

____

2 *La oficina está muy desordenada. Parece un* ***basural****.* ____________________

3 *Es diciembre, estación de Navidad. Las cajas contienen* ***campanitas y ciervos de cristal****.* ______________________________

4 *No quiero más* ***chirimbolos*** *del club de Navidad.* ____________________

5 *Ella llamó antes de* ***emprender viaje****.* ______________________________

6 *No pienso* ***hacerme cargo de*** *este monstruo.*

____

RECOGNIZING ARTISTIC EXPRESSIONS

C Metaphor—saying that a thing is something else—is often used in a description.

1 How is metaphor used to describe the desk?

____

2 How is metaphor used to describe the "action" of the disorder?

____

D Simile—saying that a thing is like something else—is expressed in Spanish by *como* or *parece*. How is simile used to describe the office?

____

READING FOR COMPREHENSION

E Read the selection again, then answer the following questions.

1 *¿Cómo se llama el protagonista de la historia?* ______________________

2 *¿En qué condición estaba su oficina cuando entró el Sr. Reeves?*

____

3 *¿Cómo estaba él?* ______________________

4 *¿Quién es Tina?* ______________________

5 *¿Qué tenía el Sr. Reeves en su agenda para ese día?*

______________________ ______________________

6 *¿Quién puede ser Shanon?* ______________________

7 *¿Quién es David?* ______________________

8 *¿Qué preocupaciones ya tiene la hermana del Sr. Reeves?*

____

La historia y la política

Cronología

España

50.000–30.000 a.C.
Evidencia de civilizaciones por yacimientos arqueológicos encontrados como *el hombre del Orce*, el *Arte Rupestre* y por las cuevas de *Cova Negra* y *Pinar*

???–600 a.C.
Ya están establecidos los íberos

600 a.C.
Llegan los celtas, se mezclan con los íberos

600–300 a.C.
Dominan los cartagineses

300 a.C.
Llega Aníbal con el ejército cartaginés

281 a.C.–200 d.C.
Llegan los romanos a conquistar

200–400
Dominan los romanos, se establece *Hispania*

409
Llegan los bárbaros

711
Invaden los moros del norte de África, se establece *Al Andalus*

1100
Época de gran prosperidad bajo Abderramán III

1469
Unen España los Reyes Católicos

América

20.000–10.000 a.C.
Inmigran los primeros habitantes por el Estrecho de Bering

2.000 a.C.–700 a.C.
Comienzan las civilizaciones en Centroamérica, México y Perú

300–800
Florecen los mayas en Centroamérica

1200–1300
Llegan los aztecas al valle de México

1200–1500
Reinan los incas en Perú

España

1473
Se introduce la imprenta en España

1492
Los Reyes Católicos conquistan Granada y terminan la dominación de los moros; mandan a Cristóbal Colón a las Indias

1517
Nombran a Carlos V emperador de España y las Indias

1519–1522
Magallanes viaja alrededor del mundo

1555–1598
Reina Felipe II

1598–1700
Pierde gran parte del Imperio bajo Felipe III, Felipe IV, Carlos II

América

1492
Llega Cristóbal Colón

1492–1521
Llegan los exploradores de Europa

1532
Llega Pizarro al Perú

1535
Establecen en México el Virreinato de Nueva España

Pizarro establece en Lima la Ciudad de los Reyes

1538
Fundan Santa Fé de Bogotá

Fundan la Universidad de Santo Tomás, en Santo Domingo, primera en el continente

1539
Fundan Asunción del Paraguay

Introducen la imprenta en México, primera en el continente

1541
Fundan Santiago de Chile

1542
Establecen la Inquisición

1544
Establecen el Virreinato del Perú

1553
Fundan la Universidad de México y la Universidad de San Marcos de Lima

1580
Establecen la ciudad de Buenos Aires

España

1700–1746
Reina Felipe V

1702–1713
Guerra de Sucesión

1759–1788
Reina Carlos III

1788–1808
Reina Carlos IV

1808–1814
Guerra de Independencia contra Napoleón

1810–1813
Guerra de Independencia de México

1811–1824
Guerras de Independencia de América del Sur

1814–1833
Reina Fernando VII

América

1717–1721
Establecen el Virreinato de Nueva Granada

1776
Establecen el Virreinato del Río de la Plata

Independencia de los Estados Unidos de América

1804
Independencia de Haití

1808
Proclaman a J. Bonaparte emperador de España y las Indias

Suprimen la Inquisición

1810
Comienzan las guerras de independencia

1813
Independencia de Paraguay y México

1815
Escribe Simón Bolívar la *Carta de Jamaica*

1816
Independencia de las Provincias Unidas del Río de la Plata

1818
Independencia de Chile

1821
Independencia de la República Dominicana

Independencia de México

1822
Independencia de Ecuador

1825
Independencia de Bolivia

España

1833–1840
Guerras Carlistas

1833–1868
Reina Isabel II

1872–1876
Guerras Carlistas

1873–1874
Se establece la República Española

1874–1885
Se restaura la monarquía;
reina Alfonso XII

América

1829
Se independiza Uruguay de las Provincias Unidas del Río de la Plata

1829–1830
Se separan Ecuador, Colombia y Venezuela de la Gran Colombia

1836
Se separa Texas de México

1844
Los Estados Unidos anexa partes de Colorado, Nuevo México, Kansas, Oklahoma y Texas

1845
Los Estados Unidos anexa Texas

1845–1848
Guerra entre México y los Estados Unidos

1848
Gana los Estados Unidos California, Utah, Nevada y partes de Arizona, Nuevo México, Colorado y Wyoming

1861
Francia interviene en México; se proclama Maximiliano como emperador

1865–1870
Guerra de Argentina, Uruguay y Brasil contra Paraguay

1867
Ejecutan al emperador Maximiliano en México

1879–1883
Guerra de Bolivia y Perú contra Chile

España

1885–1902
Sirve como reina María Cristina, madre de Alfonso XIII

1902–1931
Reina Alfonso XIII

1914–1918
España neutral

1923–1930
Gobierna el dictador Primo de Rivera

1931
Proclaman la Segunda República

1936
Comienza la Guerra Civil

1939
Triunfan los franquistas bajo el Generalísimo Francisco Franco

1939–1945
Segunda Guerra Mundial

1959
Se funda la ETA en el País Vasco

América

1888
Terminan la esclavitud en Brasil

1889
Se reúnen en Washington, D.C. los países panamericanos en la primera conferencia de los Estados Americanos

1898
España pierde Cuba, Puerto Rico y las Filipinas en la guerra contra los Estados Unidos

1902
Se independiza Cuba

1903
Se independiza Panamá de Colombia

1910–1920
Revolución mexicana

1914
Se abre el canal de Panamá

1914–1918
Primera Guerra Mundial

1930
Empieza la dictadura de Rafael Trujillo en la República Dominicana

1933–1938
Guerra entre Bolivia y Paraguay

1934
Se establece el Partido Revolucionario Institucional en México

1939–1945
Segunda Guerra Mundial

1946–1955
Gobierna Juan Perón en Argentina

1959
Empieza el comunismo en Cuba bajo Fidel Castro

España

1973
Asesinan al Primer Ministro Luis Carrero Blanco

1975
Se muere Franco

1977
Se reestablece la democracia

1978
Se establece la nueva constitución

1980
Calvo Sotelo es presidente

América

1960
Se establece el Mercado Común Centroamericano

1961
Se muere Rafael Trujillo en la República Dominicana

1965
Empieza la guerra civil en Colombia

1966
Se establece gobierno militar en Argentina

1968
Se establece gobierno militar en Perú

1969
Se establece gobierno militar en Bolivia

1970–1973
Se establece gobierno comunista en Chile bajo Salvador Allende

1973
Asesinan a Allende en un golpe militar en Chile; el General Augusto Pinochet asume control del gobierno

Juan Perón gobierna de nuevo en Argentina

1976
Se establece gobierno militar en Argentina

1977
El presidente estadounidense Jimmy Carter firma tratados con el General Omar Torrijos, iniciando el proceso para devolver el canal a Panamá

1979
Revolución en Nicaragua;
se establece gobierno comunista bajo Daniel Ortega, jefe de la junta sandinista

España

1982
Felipe González, del Partido Socialista Español, es presidente

1985
España entra en la OTAN

1986
España ingresa en la Comunidad Europea

1992
Expo en Sevilla; las Olimpíadas en Barcelona

1996
Gana la presidencia José María Aznar, del Partido Popular

América

1982
Guerrean Argentina e Inglaterra por las Islas Malvinas

Gabriel García Márquez, colombiano, gana el Premio Nobel de Literatura

1983
Se reestablece la democracia en Argentina; Carlos Menem es presidente

1984
Daniel Ortega es elegido como presidente de Nicaragua; lo oponen las guerrillas "contra" y el gobierno de los Estados Unidos

1989
Los Estados Unidos invade Panamá

1991
Firman el Tratado del Mercosur (Mercado Común del Sur) en Paraguay

Nueva constitución en Colombia

1992
Se elimina el Sendero Luminoso en Perú bajo la presidencia de Alberto Fujimori

1993
Firman el Tratado de Libre Comercio (NAFTA) los Estados Unidos, Canadá y México

1998
Se establece nueva constitución en Venezuela

Pinochet jura como Senador en el Congreso Nacional de Chile

1999
Fernando de la Rúa es presidente de Argentina

España

2000
El juez Baltazar Garzón pide la detención de Pinochet y da lugar a un debate internacional

2002
El euro se estrena en España y en otros países europeos

América

2000
México es el primer país latinoamericano que firma un acuerdo de libre comercio (ALC) con la Unión Europea

Chile solicita incorporación al Mercosur

Se retira Fujimori en Perú y se escapa a Japón

2001
Asume la presidencia de México Vicente Fox (PAN); por primera vez desde 1934 México cuenta con un presidente no perteneciente al PRI (Partido Revolucionario Institucional)

Alejandro Toledo es presidente de Perú

Ordenan arresto de Pinochet—luego lo sobreseen por razones de salud

2001–2002
Crisis financiera en Argentina; de la Rúa se retira de la presidencia; regresan los peronistas con Duhalde como presidente

EJERCICIO

SCANNING FOR INFORMATION

A Study the time line carefully, then answer the following questions.

1 Which lasted longer, the Roman domination in Spain or the Mayan civilization in Central America? ______________________

2 How long was Spain under Moorish rule? ______________________

3 For what reasons is 1492 an important date?

____

____

4 Where were the Incas, and how long had their civilization dominated when the Spaniards arrived? ______________________

5 Who was emperor of Spain when Pizarro went to Perú? ______________

6 Where was the first university established in the Americas?

____

7 When was the printing press introduced in México? ___________

8 How many viceroyalties were established in the Americas? ___________

9 What were the first Spanish-speaking countries to win independence?

______________________ ______________________

10 What was happening in Spain when the first countries gained their independence? ______________________________

11 What did México lose in the war with the United States?

____

12 Who was Maximiliano? ______________________________

13 Who was the first king of Spain after the monarchy was restored?

____

14 How did Puerto Rico become part of the United States?

____

15 What happened in México, Cuba, and Panamá during the reign of Alfonso XIII? ____

____

16 What government came to power at the end of the Spanish Civil War?

____

17 How long had Juan Perón been out of office when he returned to power?

____

18 Which countries in the Americas have had communist governments?

______________________ ______________________

____

19 What happened in Spain in 1977–1978?

____

20 What important trade agreements have been established in the Americas?

_________________________ _________________________

_________________________ _________________________

Celebrando la independencia

Con gran orgullo, Bolivia festeja el 6 de agosto su independencia de España, lograda en el año 1825. Lo que antes tenía el nombre Alto Perú hoy se conoce como Bolivia y tiene su capital en la ciudad de La Paz.

Este país fue liberado del dominio español por uno de los personajes más significativos de la historia latinoamericana: Simón Bolívar.

En un momento juró Bolívar a su maestro:

«Juro delante de usted, juro por el Dios de mis padres, juro por mi honor y mi patria, que no daré descanso a mi brazo ni reposo a mi alma hasta que haya roto las cadenas que nos oprimen por voluntad del poder español».

Promesa cumplida.

Los bolivianos no solamente festejan su independencia, sino también el gran orgullo que sienten por sus costumbres, sus tradiciones y su gente. La celebración se lleva a cabo en la Casa de la Independencia de Bolivia, que fue donde se firmó el documento que liberó el territorio en aquel glorioso 6 de agosto de 1825. Se hace una sesión de honor a la cual asiste el presidente de la República. Asiste también todo el gabinete y las autoridades más importantes. Después se lleva a cabo una misa católica y en las calles hay desfiles de escolares y de trabajadores frente al altar patrio, que se monta con las imágenes de Simón Bolívar y el Mariscal Sucre.

En las casas se reúnen con los familiares y los amigos y celebran con los platillos típicos de la región. Son muy bailadores los bolivianos y no hay fiesta que no termine con un gran baile, así que también durante la independencia se baila en las reuniones la música popular, es decir, la música folclórica.

www.EsMas.com.

EJERCICIOS

USING COGNATES TO DETERMINE MEANING

A Write the Spanish words from the selection that are cognates of the following English words.

Nouns

1	authority	________	8	history	________
2	cabinet	________	9	honor	________
3	capital	________	10	independence	________
4	celebration	________	11	moment	________
5	custom	________	12	session	________
6	document	________	13	territory	________
7	dominion	________	14	tradition	________

Adjectives

1	glorious	________	3	significant	________
2	important	________	4	typical	________

Verbs

1	celebrate	________	2	liberate	________

Beware of false cognates. Following are Spanish words with their true English meaning.

personaje/persona importante	character/personage
personaje	character (in a play)
tipo	character (joker)
carácter	character (temperament)
(de buena/mala) reputación	(of good/bad) character

B Complete the following sentences.

1 *¿Quiénes son los* ________ (characters) *más importantes en la obra de teatro?*

2 *Nos reímos mucho con Rafael: es un* ________ (character) *muy divertido.*

3 *Tengo mucha confianza en este candidato, es una persona de buena* ________ (character).

4 *Bolívar fue un* ________ (character) *muy importante en la historia de las Américas.*

USING CONTEXT TO DETERMINE MEANING

C Read the following sentences, then write the meaning of the words that appear in bold type.

1 *Con gran **orgullo**, Bolivia **festeja** su independencia de España, **lograda** en el año 1825.*

________________ ________________ ________________

2 *Son muy **bailadores** los bolivianos—todas las fiestas terminan con un baile.*

____

3 ***Juro** por mi honor y mi patria.* ________________

4 ***Sienten** un gran orgullo por sus costumbres, sus tradiciones y su gente.*

____

5 *El presidente va a **firmar** el documento.* ________________

6 *El presidente va a **asistir** a una sesión de honor.* ________________

7 *Muchas personas asisten a la **misa** católica.* ________________

8 *El Día de Independencia siempre marchan los **escolares** en un **desfile** en la calle principal.* ________________ ________________

9 *Los amigos se van a **reunir** en la casa después del desfile.*

____

UNDERSTANDING PHRASE PATTERNS

The construction *se* + third-person verb can be used to express action without saying who is performing the action, often implying that it is action performed by most people.

***Se come** pavo el día de Thanksgiving.*	Turkey is eaten at Thanksgiving./ Most people eat turkey on Thanksgiving Day.
***Se comen** otros platos tradicionales.*	Other traditional dishes are eaten./ We/they eat other traditional dishes.
***Se vende** el periódico en la farmacia.*	The newspaper is sold at the drugstore./You can get the newspaper at the drugstore.
***Se venden** los cosméticos en la farmacia.*	Cosmetics are sold at the drugstore./ They sell cosmetics at the drugstore.

The same construction can be used in other tenses.

***Se vendió** la casa.*	The house was sold.
***Se vendieron** todas las casas.*	All the houses were sold.

D Write the English meaning of the following sentences.

1 *Alto Perú hoy se conoce como Bolivia.*

____

2 *La Casa de la Independencia es el lugar donde se firmó el documento.*

____

3 *Se hace una sesión de honor.*

____

4 *Se monta el altar con las imágenes de Bolívar y Sucre.*

____

5 *En las casas se reúnen con los amigos y familiares.*

____

6 *Se baila en las reuniones.*

____

USING PHRASE PATTERNS AND CONTEXT CLUES TO DETERMINE MEANING

E Read the following sentences.

Se lleva a cabo *una misa católica en la catedral.*
La celebración ***se lleva a cabo*** *en la Casa de la Independencia.*

What does *llevar a cabo* mean? ______________

READING FOR COMPREHENSION

F Read the entire selection again, then answer the following questions.

1 When is Bolivia's Independence Day? ______________

2 What was Bolivia formerly named? ______________

3 What is Bolivia's capital city? ______________

4 Who is the national hero? ______________

5 Where do the official celebrations take place?

____

6 Who attends the memorial service?

____

7 What happens after the memorial service? ______________

8 How do people celebrate at home? ______________

Ayuda humanitaria

Un cargamento de once toneladas de ayuda humanitaria procedente de Venezuela para los heridos en el incendio que el 29 de diciembre causó la muerte de 280 personas en Lima, llegó a Lima en un avión militar. El cargamento arribó, esta tarde, al aeropuerto internacional "Jorge Chávez" y fue entregado en ese mismo lugar a funcionarios del Instituto Nacional de Defensa Civil (INDECI) por representantes de la embajada venezolana. La donación consiste en 133 cajas que contienen medicamentos, material quirúrgico y ropa de cama especiales para el tratamiento de personas quemadas, según un informe detallado del envío que fue entregado a los periodistas. El ministro consejero de la embajada de Venezuela, Ricardo Alfonso, afirmó que "esta es una ayuda del Gobierno de la República Bolivariana de Venezuela, que se solidariza con el pueblo peruano por el incendio que ha dejado damnificados a un gran número de hermanos andinos". "Hemos traído esta ayuda cumpliendo un encargo expreso del presidente constitucional de nuestro país, Hugo Chávez", añadió según precisa EFE. El cargamento fue recibido por el capitán de navío de la armada peruana Arístides Mussio, subjefe del INDECI, quien lo entregó en el mismo lugar a delegados del Ministerio de Salud que harán llegar la donación a los hospitales donde son atendidos los heridos.

EJERCICIOS

SKIMMING FOR MEANING

A Read the selection quickly, then answer the following questions.

1 What country is receiving aid? ______________________

2 What country is sending assistance? ______________________

Radioprogramas del Perú, S.A.

USING WORD FORMATION TO DETERMINE MEANING

The past participle of a verb can be identified by its suffix: *-ado/-ido/-to*.

afectar	to affect	*afectado*	affected
entregar	to deliver	*entregado*	delivered
herir	to wound	*herido*	wounded
quemar	to burn	*quemado*	burned
atender	to assist	*atendido*	assisted
damnificar	to harm	*damnificado*	harmed

When the participle follows a form of *haber*, it indicates action that occurred recently.

El incendio ha afectado a muchas personas.	The fire affected a lot of people.

The participle can also be used as a noun or adjective to indicate the results of an action.

Muchas personas fueron heridas.	A lot of people were wounded.
Llevaron a los heridos al hospital.	They took the wounded (ones) to the hospital.

B Find the following expressions in the selection and write the English meaning of the words that appear in bold type.

1 *El cargamento* ***fue entregado****...* ______________________

2 *el tratamiento de* ***personas quemadas****...* ______________________

3 *el incendio ha dejado* ***damnificados*** *a nuestros hermanos...*

____

4 ***Hemos traído*** *esta ayuda...* ______________________

5 *El cargamento* ***fue recibido****...* ______________________

6 ***Los heridos son atendidos*** *en los hospitales.* ______________________

SCANNING FOR DETAILS

C Read the selection carefully, then answer the following questions.

1 When and where did the fire occur? ______________________

2 How many people died in the fire? ______________________

3 How much did the aid shipment weigh? ______________________

4 How was it sent? ______________________

5 Who delivered the shipment, and what organization received it?

____

6 What did the shipment contain?

____

El Canal de Panamá

El Canal de Panamá es como una de las maravillas de ingeniería del mundo. Aun con los adelantos de hoy es asombroso observar cómo un enorme barco de contenedores se desliza a través de las esclusas para cruzar de un océano a otro. El Canal tiene aproximadamente 50 millas de largo y para completar el tránsito, los barcos son elevados a una altura de 85 pies por medio de tres juegos de esclusas. El Canal en sí se transita en ocho horas, pero las naves permanecen de catorce a dieciséis horas en aguas territoriales. Llama extraordinariamente la atención la operación del Canal por su eficiencia, a pesar de haberse construido al inicio del siglo XX.

Pero la historia comenzó muchos años atrás. En 1524 el Rey de España, Carlos V, ordenó estudiar la posibilidad de construir una ruta a través del Istmo, pero se presumió que no se avanzó al estimar que machetes no servirían para la tarea.

En 1821 Panamá se independizó de España y se unió voluntariamente a Colombia. En 1880 los franceses iniciaron los trabajos de excavación para construir un canal por el Istmo bajo la dirección del Conde Fernando de Lesseps, constructor del Canal de Suez, pero 20 años después de luchar con la selva, enfermedades y serios problemas financieros se vieron forzados a abandonar el enorme proyecto.

El 3 de noviembre de 1903 Panamá se separó de Colombia y surgió como república independiente. Ese mismo año (el 18 de noviembre) se firmó en Washington el tratado concediéndole a los Estados Unidos la autorización para construir un canal por el territorio panameño.

El 15 de agosto de 1914, el carguero norteamericano *Ancón* hizo la primera travesía por el Canal.

El 1° de octubre de 1979, el famoso Canal de Panamá entró en otra etapa de su historia. De acuerdo con los tratados firmados por el entonces Jefe de Gobierno de Panamá General Omar Torrijos Herrera (q.e.p.d.)* y el Presidente de los Estados Unidos Jimmy Carter el 7 de septiembre de 1977, en Washington, la "Zona del Canal" de 10 millas

---

www.focuspublicationsint.com.

**q.e.p.d.* is an abbreviation for *qué en paz descanse* "may he/she rest in peace."

de ancho y 50 de largo, comenzó a revertir a Panamá. El proceso de entregar el Canal y toda su infraestructura en la antigua Zona del Canal tomó 20 años y concluyó el 1° de enero del año 2000.

El peaje promedio que pagan los barcos por transitar el Canal es alrededor de $29.000, pero muchos de ellos se ahorran hasta diez veces esa cifra al eliminar el viaje alrededor del Cabo de Hornos. Como dato interesante podemos mencionar que el *Rapsody of the Seas* ostenta el récord de haber pagado la cifra más alta, $165.235,58, mientras el señor Richard Halliburton aún mantiene el suyo por haber pagado en 1926 la cifra más baja, 0,36 centésimos, cuando se le calculó su desplazamiento para cruzar el Canal nadando.

EJERCICIOS

SKIMMING FOR MEANING

This selection contains many Spanish words that have English cognates. Even when you read through the selection quickly, cognates make it much easier to get an idea of its overall meaning.

USING CONTEXT TO GUESS MEANING

The following words may be new to you.

NOUNS

adelantados	*carguero*	*cifra*
esclusas	*travesía*	*desplazamiento*
juegos de esclusas	*etapa*	
tarea	*peaje*	

VERBS

deslizarse	*firmar*	*ahorrar*
surgir	*entregar*	

A Read these words in context, then write the meaning of each one in the space provided.

1 *Aun con los* ***adelantados*** *de hoy es asombroso observar la maravilla de ingeniería del Canal.* ____________________

2 *Los enormes barcos de contenedores* ***se deslizan*** *a través de* ***las esclusas*** *para cruzar de un océano a otro.* ________________ ________________

3 *Los barcos son elevados por medio de tres* ***juegos de esclusas****.*

____

4 *Los machetes no sirven para* **la tarea** *de construir un canal.*

____

5 *Panamá se separó de Colombia y* **surgió** *como república independiente.*

____

6 *El* **carguero** *norteamericano* Ancón *hizo la primera* **travesía** *por el Canal.*

______________________ ______________________

7 *En 1979, el Canal entró en otra* **etapa** *de su historia.* ______________________

8 *Los tratados fueron* **firmados** *por el General Omar Torrijos Herrera y el Presidente Jimmy Carter.* ______________________

9 *El proceso de* **entregar** *el Canal tomó 20 años.* ______________________

10 *El* **peaje** *promedio que pagan los barcos por transitar el Canal es $29.000.*

____

11 *Muchos barcos* **ahorran** *diez veces esta* **cifra** *al eliminar el viaje alrededor del Cabo de Hornos.* ______________________ ______________________

12 *Sólo pagó 36 centésimos por su* **desplazamiento** *para cruzar el Canal nadando.* ______________________

READING NUMBERS

B Look at the numbers mentioned in the selection, then tell how they are written differently in Spanish and English.

____

____

SCANNING FOR DETAILS

C Read the selection carefully to find the answers to the following questions. Write the answers in the space provided.

1 What political leader made the first attempt to study the possibility of building a canal in Panama? When was that? ______________________

2 What expertise did el Conde Fernando de Lesseps bring to the project? What country sponsored him?

____

3 Why did they give up? ______________________

4 When did Panama become an independent republic? What else happened that same year? ______________________

5 What was the name of the first ship to cross the Canal? ______________________

6 What happened in 1979? Who signed the treaty?

____

7 How long did the transfer of the Canal from the United States to Panama take? ____________

8 What is the average toll for crossing the Canal? ____________

9 What is the highest toll ever paid? What is the lowest?

____

Puente binacional

Los presidentes de Bolivia, Jorge Quiroga, y de Perú, Alejandro Toledo, inaugurarán el próximo 27 de enero un puente binacional en la carretera que une ambas naciones, en el marco de la visita de 3 días que el mandatario peruano inicia al país en esa fecha. El puente de 106 metros, construido con recursos provenientes de un crédito de la Corporación Andina de Fomento (CAF), sustituirá una antigua estructura que vincula ambos territorios y favorecerá una mayor fluidez y seguridad del tráfico vehicular, informó este lunes el Servicio de Caminos de Bolivia. Toledo ingresará a territorio boliviano por la localidad de Desaguadero, a orillas del lago Titicaca que comparten Bolivia y Perú, donde ambos presidentes y sus respectivos gabinetes se reunirán el mismo 27. Los presidentes analizarán durante su encuentro varios temas de interés bilateral, principalmente aquellos proyectos que tienen que ver con el desarrollo integral del sur de Perú y occidente de Bolivia. La exportación de gas natural boliviano a la costa norte del Pacífico será otro tema que abordarán los mandatarios, dado el interés que el millonario proyecto ha despertado tanto en Perú como en Chile, cuyos puertos se constituyen en alternativa para la salida del gas. Por otra parte, Quiroga y Toledo pondrán en marcha un plan de seguro indígena con un crédito de 35 millones de dólares del Banco Mundial que permitirá la atención de 2 millones de personas que viven en áreas rurales en torno a la frontera de ambos países.

EJERCICIOS

SKIMMING FOR GENERAL MEANING

A Read the selection quickly, then answer the following questions.

1 What two countries are planning a joint project?

____

2 What is the project? ____

Radioprogramas del Perú, S.A.

USING WORD FORMATION TO DETERMINE MEANING

The future tense is used in Spanish to indicate projected future action. It is formed by adding the following suffixes to the infinitive of the verb.

yo	*-é*	*nosotros/-as*	*-emos*
tú	*-ás*		
usted/él/ella	*-á*	*ustedes/ellos/-as*	*-án*

hablaré/comeré/escribiré	*hablaremos/comeremos/escribiremos*
hablarás/comerás/escribirás	
hablará/comerá/escribirá	*hablarán/comerán/escribirán*

A few verbs use irregular base forms instead of the infinitive to form the future tense.

tener	*tendr-*	*poner*	*pondr-*	*salir*	*saldr-*	*venir*	*vendr-*
poder	*podr-*	*saber*	*sabr-*	*querer*	*querr-*		
decir	*dir-*	*hacer*	*har-*				

B Find the future tense forms in the selection that correspond to the following English phrases; write the form in the space provided.

1 they will inaugurate ____________________

2 it will replace ____________________

3 he will enter ____________________

4 they will meet ____________________

5 they will analyze ____________________

6 it will be ____________________

7 they will discuss ____________________

8 they will start up ____________________

9 it will permit ____________________

READING FOR DETAILS

C Read the selection again, then answer the following questions.

1 Who is the President of Bolivia? Who is the President of Perú?

____

2 Which one is visiting the other's country? ____________________

3 What are they inaugurating, and on what date?

____

4 Who is funding the project? ____________________

5 What will its benefits be? ____________________

6 What other topics will be discussed at this meeting? ____________________

____

La pacifista

Ana Teresa Bernal ha dedicado años a luchar contra la guerra. Es la coordinadora de la Semana por la Paz desde el 8 de septiembre. Cuando vio por televisión cómo desaparecía bajo las llamas el antiguo Palacio de Justicia y oyó a los magistrados rogar por sus vidas, Ana Teresa Bernal se prometió a sí misma que apostaría todas sus fuerzas a luchar por la paz y contra la guerra.

Un año después, en frente de ese palacio, artistas de todo el país tapizaron la plaza con flores y con un gran concierto dieron a luz el Movimiento por la Vida. Desde finales de los 80 Ana Teresa lideró ese grupo, que luchó por rescatar la vida en medio de tantos muertos. Una gran cena nacional, una vuelta a Colombia y cientos de foros fueron algunas de sus estrategias. A principios de los 90 el movimiento perdió intensidad pero se transformó en la Red de Iniciativas Ciudadanas por la Paz y contra la Guerra (Redepaz), que bajo la batuta de Ana Teresa coordina todos los años desde 1994 la Semana por la Paz.

Son cinco días, desde el 8 de septiembre hasta el 13, en que el país habla más de paz que de guerra, piensa más en cómo hacerles resistencia a los guerreros que en cómo fortalecerlos y asume iniciativas ciudadanas para coger las riendas del país y para no delegar a otros las decisiones sobre el futuro de Colombia.

Apostarle a la vida, a la paz, a Eros, no es fácil. Para ello toca volver a empezar todos los días. Cuando Ana Teresa lideró en 1997, junto con otras organizaciones, el Mandato Ciudadano por la Paz, por lo menos 10 millones de colombianos votaron a favor de la solución política a la guerra. Hoy son muchos menos los que creen en ella con igual fuerza.

Pero esta bogotana de 42 años no se desanima. Hija de la famosa torera Teresita Montañez, heredó de su madre el coraje para capotear a los pesimistas y trabajar con los que sólo le tienen miedo a una guerra de verdad. Tuvo dos influencias grandes en su vida: la de un hippy pensador y la de un activista de la Juco. Del primero aprendió

Semana, 27 de agosto de 2001, p. 63. Reproducida aquí con el permiso de *Semana Magazine*, Colombia.

la irreverencia, la pasión por lo bello y la forma de cambiar las costumbres sin recurrir a la violencia. Del segundo, la eficacia de la política.

A los 13 años Ana Teresa parecía más una monjita de izquierda que una adolescente. Mientras sus compañeras iban a fiestas ella leía a Marx, a Lenin y a Mao. Aún en su uniforme de colegiala repartía volantes en las calles que invitaban a los trabajadores a la revolución y enfurecía a sus vecinos con las filas de niños de la calle que enfilaban por su apartamento para que ella les enseñara a escribir.

A los 20 años se casó pero muy pronto se aburrió de ser ama de casa y volvió con toda la fuerza al activismo político. Se vinculó a Firmes, coqueteó con el M-19, fue candidata a la Asamblea Constituyente y ahora es delegada del gobierno en el Comité temático de los diálogos con las FARC. Pero su mayor aporte ha sido impulsar el movimiento pacifista en Colombia. Desde Redepaz ha impulsado talleres de educación para la convivencia, ha sentado en la misma mesa a las víctimas de los grupos armados para que trabajen de la mano contra la guerra en busca de cumplir su gran sueño: *Que seamos capaces de cambiar este país sin matarnos.*

EJERCICIOS

SKIMMING FOR GENERAL MEANING

A Read the entire selection quickly, then answer the following questions.

1 Whom is this selection about? ______________________________

2 How would you describe her? ______________________________

3 What is her goal? ______________________________

USING WORD FORMATION TO DETERMINE MEANING

The preterite tense is used to relate events that began and ended in the past. The third-person preterite is formed as follows.

-ar verbs	infinitive form minus *-ar* + *-ó/-aron*
-er/-ir verbs	infinitive form minus *-er/-ir* + *-ió/-ieron*

The forms for *ser* and *ir* are *fue/fueron*; the forms for *tener* are *tuvo/tuvieron*.

B Find the preterite forms of the following verbs in the selection and write each form below, along with the subject of the verb (performer of the action).

		PRETERITE FORM	SUBJECT
1	*ver*	______________	______________
2	*oír*	______________	______________
3	*prometerse*	______________	______________
4	*tapizar*	______________	______________
5	*dar a luz*	______________	______________
6	*liderar*	______________	______________
7	*luchar*	______________	______________
8	*ser*	______________	______________
9	*perder*	______________	______________
10	*transformarse*	______________	______________
11	*votar*	______________	______________
12	*tener*	______________	______________
13	*aprender*	______________	______________
14	*casarse*	______________	______________
15	*aburrirse*	______________	______________
16	*volver*	______________	______________
17	*vincularse*	______________	______________
18	*coquetear*	______________	______________

The imperfect tense is used to describe two kinds of past action, which are translated quite differently into English. The third-person singular imperfect is formed as follows.

-ar verbs   infinitive form minus *-ar* + *-aba*
-er/-ir verbs   infinitive form minus *-er/-ir* + *-ía*

The form for *ir* is *iba*; the form for *ser* is *era*.

In a narrative, or recounting of an event, background action—action that started before the preterite event or that continues to occur at the same time—is expressed by the imperfect.

Cuando volvió a su casa, vio que los niños la ***esperaban****.*   When she returned home, she saw that the children **were waiting** for her.

In a description of the past, actions that were performed customarily or that depict a way of life are expressed by the imperfect.

*Cuando era adolescente, los niños la **esperaban** todos los días.*	When she was a teenager, the children **waited/used to wait/would wait** for her every day.

C Complete the following sentences.

1 *Cuando vio la televisión,* ______________ (was going up in flames) *el Palacio de Justicia.*

2 *A los trece años* ______________ (she looked more like) *una monjita que una adolescente.*

3 *Mientras sus amigas* ______________ (went) *a fiestas, ella* ______________ (read).

4 *Ana Teresa* ______________ (would distribute) *volantes en las calles.*

5 *Esto* ______________ (used to infuriate) *a los vecinos.*

6 *Los niños* ______________ (lined up) *por su apartamento.*

The subjunctive is used to express a wish or hoped-for outcome in the future.

Present subjunctive forms typically change the *-a* of *-ar* verbs to *-e* and the *-e* of *-er*/*-ir* verbs to *-a*.

pensar	*piensa*	she thinks	*piense*	she might think
volver	*vuelve*	he returns	*vuelva*	he might return
aburrirse	*se aburren*	they get bored	*se aburran*	they might get bored

Subjunctive forms are almost always preceded by *que* and sometimes by *para que*.

*Ella los reúne **para que** hablen.*	She gets them together so that they will/might talk.
*Ella lo llama **para que** vote.*	She calls him to get him to vote.
***Que** voten todos.*	May everyone vote./Let's hope everyone votes.

D Complete the following sentences.

1 *Ana Teresa reúne a las víctimas para que* ______________ (will work) *juntos.*

2 *Los niños la esperan para que les* ______________ (will teach) *a leer.*

3 *¡Qué* ______________ (long live) *la revolución!*

Past subjunctive forms typically end in *-ara/-aras/-ara/-áramos/-aran* for *-ar* verbs and *-iera/-ieras/-iera/-iéramos/-ieran* for *-er/-ir* verbs.

pensar	*pensara*	she would/could/might think
volver	*volviéramos*	we would/could/might return
aburrirse	*se aburrieran*	they would/could/might get bored

Ella los reunió para que hablaran. She got them together so they would talk.

Ella lo llamó para que votara. She called him so he would vote.

E Complete the following sentences.

1 *Ana Teresa los reunió para que* ________________ *juntos.*
would work

2 *Los niños la esperaban para que les* ________________ *a leer.*
could teach

USING A SPANISH-SPANISH DICTIONARY

When you look up a word in a Spanish-only dictionary, you will usually find a definition that you understand or an English cognate that will guide you to the word's meaning.

aportar · *contribuir*
la aportación/el aporte · *la contribución*
impulsar · *estimular*
el impulso · *el estímulo*
apostar · *poner en una situación/arriesgar*
el volante · *hoja de papel que se distribuye en la calle para comunicar algo/rueda que se usa para conducir una máquina/tira de tela fruncida que sirve para decorar la ropa*
la convivencia · *la coexistencia/la habilidad de vivir juntos en paz*

F Using words from the list above, complete the following sentences.

1 *Bolívar* ________________ *la vida por la patria.*
risked

2 *El mayor* ________________ *de Ana Teresa ha sido*
contribution

________________ *el movimiento pacifista en Colombia.*
to stimulate

3 *Cuando joven, repartía* ________________ *en las calles.*
flyers

4 ________________ *tiene que ser posible en todas partes del mundo.*
Peaceful coexistence

5 *Maneja muy bien, pues sabe usar* ________________.
the steering wheel

6 *Mi amiga es muy femenina y a ella le gusta usar vestidos y blusas con*

________________.
ruffles

USING CONTEXT TO DETERMINE MEANING

G Read the following sentences, then write the meaning of the words that appear in bold type.

1 *Los magistrados* ***rogaron*** *por sus vidas.* ____________________

2 *Ella decidió* ***luchar*** *por la paz y contra la guerra.* ____________________

3 *Los artistas* ***tapizaron*** *la plaza con flores.* ____________________

4 *La futura madre salió para el hospital a las tres y* ***dio a luz*** *a un precioso bebé a las cuatro y media.* ____________________

5 *Con flores y un concierto,* ***dieron a luz*** *el Movimiento por la Vida.*

____

6 *Los bomberos apagaron las* ***llamas*** *y* ***rescataron*** *a muchas personas.*

____________________ ____________________

7 *Ana Teresa luchó por* ***rescatar la vida*** *del grupo.* ____________________

8 *El director de la orquesta marcaba el ritmo con su* ***batuta****.*

____

9 *El grupo coordina cada año la Semana por la Paz, bajo la* ***batuta*** *de Ana Teresa.* ____________________

10 *El hombre montó al caballo,* ***cogió las riendas*** *y se fue.*

____

11 *Para no delegar a otros las decisiones importantes, es necesario* ***coger las riendas*** *del país.* ____________________

12 *No lo hice bien la primera vez. Voy a* ***volver a empezar****.*

____

13 *Para hacer eso, ella tiene que* ***volver a empezar*** *todos los días.*

____

14 *Ella tiene mucho entusiasmo, nunca* ***se desanima****.* ____________________

15 *Su madre era torera y sabía* ***capotear****, es decir, confundir al toro con los movimientos de la capa.* ____________________

16 *Ella tiene el coraje para* ***capotear*** *a los pesimistas.*

____

17 *Es mejor resolver los problemas sin* ***recurrir*** *al terrorismo.*

____

18 *Ella aprendió la forma de cambiar las costumbres sin* ***recurrir*** *a la violencia.*

____

READING FOR COMPREHENSION

H Read the entire selection again, then answer the following questions.

1 *¿Qué coordina Ana Teresa Bernal?* ______________________

2 *¿Con qué organizaciones ha trabajado?*

______________________ ______________________

______________________ ______________________

____

3 *¿Cuándo se lleva a cabo la Semana por la Paz?*

____

4 *¿Qué hacen durante la Semana por la Paz?*

____

____

5 *¿Qué aprendió de su vida como "hippy"?*

____

____

6 *¿Qué posición tiene con el gobierno?*

____

7 *¿Qué significa "Redepaz"?*

____

8 *¿Cuál es su gran sueño?*

____

Una conversación entre marido y mujer

—¿Cómo hago, Chinita? —se disculpó el marido—. Me paso el día contestando las cartas que te mandan a vos. Son más de tres mil cartas, y en todas te piden algo: una beca para los hijos, ajuares de novia, juegos de dormitorio, trabajos de sereno, qué sé yo. Tenés que levantarte rápido antes de que yo también me enferme.

—No te hagas el gracioso. Sabés que mañana o pasado me voy a morir. Si te pido que vengas es porque necesito encargarte algunas cosas.

—Pedíme lo que quieras.

—No abandones a los pobres, a mis grasitas. Todos estos que andan por aquí lamiéndote los zapatos te van a dar vuelta la cara algún día. Pero los pobres no, Juan. Son los únicos que saben ser fieles. —El marido le acarició el pelo. Ella le apartó las manos: —Hay una sola cosa que no te voy a perdonar.

—Que me case de nuevo —trató de bromear él.

—Cásate las veces que quieras. Para mí, mejor. Así vas a darte cuenta de lo que has perdido. Lo que no quiero es que la gente me olvide, Juan. No dejes que me olviden.

—Quedáte tranquila. Ya está todo arreglado. No te van a olvidar.

—Claro. Ya está todo arreglado —repitió Evita.

EJERCICIOS

USING WORD FORMATION TO DETERMINE MEANING

Affirmative commands are given in the present indicative when directed at someone addressed as *tú*. Object and reflexive pronouns are added to the end of these commands.

Llama a mi madre. Llámala.	Call my mother. Call her.
Ayuda a tu hermano. Ayúdalo.	Help your brother. Help him.
Siéntate aquí.	Sit here.

Tomás Eloy Martínez, *Santa Evita*, pp. 14–15.

A Find the commands in the selection that correspond to the following English commands and write them below.

1 Get married. ____________________________

2 Stay calm. ____________________________

Negative commands are given in the present subjunctive. Object and reflexive pronouns go between the *no* and the verb.

No llames a mi madre. No la llames.	Don't call my mother. Don't call her.
No ayudes a tu hermano. No lo ayudes.	Don't help your brother. Don't help him.
No te sientes aquí.	Don't sit here.

B Find the commands in the selection that correspond to the following English commands and write them below.

1 Don't abandon the poor people.

____

2 Don't be funny.

____

3 Don't let them forget me.

____

The following expressions followed by the gerund form of a verb indicate weariness or slight disdain for the activity mentioned.

pasarse el día* ________ *-ndo

Se pasa el día viendo telenovelas.	She spends the whole day watching soap operas.

anda* ________ *-ndo

Anda diciendo que es el mejor de la clase.	He goes around saying that he's the best in the class.

C Find the expressions in the selection that correspond to the following English expressions and write them below.

1 Those who go around licking your boots (shoes)

____

2 I spend the day answering the letters they send to you.

____

RECOGNIZING VARIETIES OF SPANISH

Several forms of expression in this selection are typically Argentine.

- The use of *vos* and its corresponding verb forms for *tú*

  Tenés *que levantarte.*
  Sabés *que me voy a morir.*
  Pedíme *lo que quieras.*

- The expression *qué sé yo*—a conversation filler similar to "y'know" or "I dunno"

READING FOR COMPREHENSION

D Practice your reading skills to determine the meaning of unfamiliar words, read the entire selection again, and answer the following questions.

1 *¿Cuál es el nombre de cariño que el marido usa para su mujer?*

____

2 *¿Cuántas cartas recibe esta mujer?* ____________________

3 *¿Qué le piden para sus hijos?* ____________________

—para sus bodas? ____________________

—para sus casas? ____________________

4 *¿Cómo está la mujer?* ____________________

5 *¿Qué le aconseja a su esposo?* ____________________

6 *Según ella, ¿quiénes son las personas fieles?* ____________________

7 *¿Qué le pide ella a su esposo?* ____________________

8 *¿Quiénes son este marido y mujer?* ____________________

Suggestions for further reading

1. Keep an eye out for advertisements, brochures, guides, announcements of shows and other entertainment, and newspapers published for the Hispanic community. These can often be found in the lobbies of Hispanic restaurants, on notice boards at Hispanic grocery stores, in dance studios where Latin dances are taught, and at public libraries.

2. Browse the Internet, an all-encompassing resource. The following are excellent "starting" web sites.

www.eresmas.com	Spain
www.esmas.com	Latin America
www.alltheweb.com	select the Spanish language and search the topics that interest you
www.chevere.com	Venezuela
www.terra.com	access information about 16 countries where Spanish is spoken
www.bolivia.com	Bolivia—or *www.* + the name of any country + *.com*

www.espanol.yahoo.com
www.univision.com
www.cervantesvirtual.com
www.telemundo.com

3. Look for magazines and newspapers in Spanish. The following magazines are widely available in the United States.

Acción deportiva
Cosmopolitan en español
Cristina
Latino Baseball
¡Mira!
People en español
Selecciones del Reader's Digest
Vogue

For an exhaustive list of newspapers and magazines available in Spanish, go to www.prensalatina.com.

4. Read books. If you especially liked a book excerpt here, find and read the entire book—and look on the back cover to find other books by the same author. You can also look up authors you like on www.amazon.com, where you will find book reviews and suggestions from other readers.

Check the "Libros en español" sections at local libraries and bookstores.

Look in the library or at a university bookstore for anthologies of literature. These will give you a good overview of the best-known authors of poetry, short stories, essays, and novels.

Answer key

La cocina

Guía para la buena alimentación y *Menú de México*

A 1. frutas 2. A 3. leche, calcio 4. carne, carne, pollo y pavo, huevo(s), chícharos y frijoles, pescado 5. fibra

B 1. postres 2. la ensalada, ensalada de jamón, pollo y queso, pollo en mole negro, tacos de pollo, pechuga de pollo rellena, enmoladas de pollo, suprema de pollo, consomé de pollo, fajitas de pollo 3. café americano, expresso, capuccino 4. low in calories 5. café americano 6. camarones rellenos, medallón de camarones 7. yes

C 1. consomé de pollo, tacos de carne, fajitas de pollo 2. quesadillas, tamales, tacos, carne asada a la tampiqueña, medallón de camarones, spaghetti, tacos, fajitas, hamburguesa (con pan), sándwich, pepito 3. ensalada de frutas, lentejas con plátano

Gazpacho

A 1. number 2. persons 3. time 4. preparation 5. minutes 6. ingredients 7. tomatoes 8. mature 9. anterior 10. fine 11. vinegar 12. salt 13. part 14. moment 15. serve 16. move

B of good quality/cut into very small pieces

C 1. of, from 2. with 3. without 4. in, on, at

D separately

E las hortalizas, las verduras

F 1. to make cold/to chill 2. ice 3. refrigerator

G The cook/cooks/Mexican cuisine/in the kitchen

H 1. pelados, peeled tomatoes 2. mojado, moistened bread 3. cocinadas, cooked vegetables 4. batidos, beaten eggs 5. cocidas, stewed fruit 6. asada, grilled meat 7. hervida, boiled water

I 1. spicy (hot) food 2. boiling water

J 1. The children eat well. 2. The soup is really cold. 3. The food is quite hot.

K 1. soaked bread 2. well-fried beans 3. reheat the soup

L 1. peeled, seeds, bread, the day before, crumbs, soaked in water, tureen 2. very cold, refrigerator, pieces, ice, at the last minute

M 1. poner 2. batir 3. meter 4. mover 5. servir

N 1. Se ponen las hortalizas en la batidora. 2. Se bate la mezcla. 3. Se mete la mezcla en la nevera. 4. Se ponen unos cubitos de hielo en el gazpacho. 5. Se mueve el gazpacho. 6. Se sirve el gazpacho.

Piña

A 1. "Frutas de América tropical y subtropical, historia y usos" (Fruits of Tropical and Subtropical America, their history and uses) 2. "Piña" (Pineapple) 3. receta (recipe), pastel de piña (pineapple pie) 4. past 5. a. the American continent, 1492 and later b. native American peoples before Columbus c. the New World d. the Spaniards e. the discovery of America f. New Castile—Spain's territories in the New World g. the correspondent wrote to his king

B *Nouns:* 1. error 2. animal 3. language 4. origin 5. fruit 6. part 7. garden 8. native 9. gesture 10. treasure 11. plant 12. testimony 13. cultivation *Adjectives:* 1. savage 2. exquisite 3. fragrant 4. daily 5. medicinal 6. important *Verbs:* 1. to accompany 2. to offer 3. to suffer *Adverb:* 1. rapidly

C 1. confusión, dispersión, transformación 2. a. la cultivación b. la preparación c. la provocación d. la propagación e. la imaginación

D heredad, eternidad, hospitalidad, suavidad, necesidad, ingeniosidad

E se llamaba, cultivaban, conocían, preparaban, acompañaban

F el infinitivo (the infinitive)

El cumpleaños de Frida Kahlo

A fiestas (parties)

B 1. nopales en pipián verde, estofado de frutas, pollitos a la piña 2. pescado blanco de Pátzcuaro, manitas de cerdo, pechugas de pollo en escabeche, ropa vieja 3. ensaladeras; nopalitos, cebolla, jitomate, queso; lechugas romanas, berros, aguacates, jitomates, cebolla 4. platos de barro; borracha, mexicana, tomate con cilantro, chile cascabel con jitomate asado 5. en los centros de las mesas; dulce de camote con piña, natillas, flan de piñón; cazuelas 6. manjares infantiles

C 1. crumbled 2. split or halved 3. tossed 4. roasted

D 1. treats 2. stew 3. feet 4. breasts 5. you cook/or boil 6. you measure 7. you drain 8. the burner 9. thick

E one that is cooked until it falls apart

F play a trick, candy-seller, two or three of these delicious treats

G 1. abrebotellas 2. lavaplatos, dishwasher 3. tocadiscos, record player 4. el prensapapas, potato masher

H went around placing

Pastel chabela

A 1. Tita y Nacha 2. el pastel de boda, la boda de Pedro con Rosaura 3. 180 4. 170 5. una vasija con cebo de carnero derretido 6. agosto y septiembre 7. *Answers will vary.* 8. *Answers will vary.*

La música

Discos

A 1. discos compactos 2. Son del Sur 3. It's probably better for relaxing. 4. Exciter 5. Tsanca, Labordeta 6. Tsanca 7. Ana Belén 8. Labordeta

La música y vitalidad de Compay Segundo

A 1. Compay Segundo 2. Cuba 3. 94 4. He's a singer, a composer, and an inventor. 5. Chan Chan, La Negra Tomasa, Las Flores de la Vida 6. the movie and the CD "Buena Vista Social Club"

B *Nouns:* 1. music 2. vitality 3. record 4. interest 5. composer 6. inventor 7. instrument 8. hybrid 9. guitar 10. duo 11. member 12. rhythm 13. musician 14. study, (recording) studio 15. contemporary 16. project 17. time 18. musicologist 19. base *Adjectives:* 1. famous 2. modern 3. animated 4. second 5. Caribbean 6. well-known 7. entire *Verbs:* 1. to create 2. to venerate 3. to announce 4. to affirm 5. to insist

C 1. film, película 2. group, conjunto 3. extension, prórroga 4. famous, reconocido 5. appear, surgir 6. be satisfied, conformarse

D 1. an instrument with three strings 2. ago (back) 3. he played alongside 4. replaced by 5. remained 6. recording

Los premios Grammy Latinos

A 1. Plácido Domingo, ópera 2. Pepe Aguilar, ranchera 3. Juan Esteban Aristizabal, rock 4. Christina Aguilera, pop-R&B 5. Bebel Gilberto, romántica 6. Sindicato Argentino, hip-hop 7. Luis Miguel, bolero 8. Julio Iglesias, melódica

B six

C *Sustantivos:* 1. giant 2. representative 3. tenor 4. opera 5. type 6. tribute 7. rock singer 8. nomination 9. population 10. opportunity *Adjetivos:* 1. possible 2. annual 3. professional 4. diverse 5. romantic 6. philanthropic 7. rich 8. seductive *Verbos:* 1. to nominate 2. to be of the opinion 3. to mix 4. to offer 5. to define 6. to compete 7. to include

D 1. actual 2. espectáculo 3. realmente 4. corriente

E 1. representante 2. presidente 3. residentes 4. inmigrantes 5. ayudante

F 1. la población 2. las nominaciones 3. la posición 4. las atracciones 5. la sección 6. la representación 7. las organizaciones 8. la competición

G 1. different 2. Rap music is quite different from classical music./ Rap music and classical music have nothing in common./Rap music is nothing like classical music. 3. award or prize 4. achievements

Los Rabanes

A 1. Chitré, Panamá 2. Grammy Latino for best vocal group 3. 3, Emilio Reguiera, Christian Torres, Javier Saavedra 4. el calipso, el reggae, el son haitiano, la salsa, el ritmo cubano 5. México, Puerto Rico, Estados Unidos, Europa 6. Emilio Stefan

B 1. native to or originally from 2. located 3. awarding or "handing over" 4. native to or authentic 5. achieving

Tomatito

A 1. an interview 2. flamenco 3. las bulerías, las soleás, las tarantas 4. Turkish music, jazz 5. Camarón, for almost 20 years 6. two Grammys 7. Elton John, Frank Sinatra, George Benson 8. *Pacto con el diablo, Flamenco*

B 1. la guitarrista 2. el solista 3. el saxofonista 4. la jazzista 5. la celista 6. las violinistas 7. los pianistas

C 1. because (of the fact that) 2. It's all the same to me. 3. fashionable 4. sound tracks 5. naturally, it goes without saying

El tango

A 1. Buenos Aires 2. no 3. Pope Pius X, who thought it was immoral until he saw a performance 4. Paris, New York, Tokyo 5. Buenos Aires 6. yes 7. on a tango tour of Buenos Aires 8. to the tango hotline in any big city 9. tangueros 10. milongas

Si se calla el cantor

A The singer should sing.

B 1. a song 2. hope, light, and joy 3. be a light over the fields for those below 4. silence 5. life itself

Recuerdos de la niñez

A 1. por medio de las canciones (singing songs) 2. Miss Jiménez 3. no 4. "America the Beautiful" 5. a Puerto Rico 6. la hija del mar y el sol (the daughter of the sea and the sun) 7. Cristóbal Colón (Christopher Columbus) 8. "En mi viejo San Juan"

B 1. la Guindilla 2. Sí 3. el día de la Virgen 4. 42 5. con su varita (baton) 6. porque había cambiado su voz (his voice had changed) 7. con admiración

C 1. a fin de año (at the end of the year) 2. Julius 3. Susan 4. bastante cambiado (changed quite a bit) 5. los mejores alumnos (the best students) 6. la monja de las pecas (the nun with freckles) 7. de nervios (nerves) 8. con mucho sentimiento (with a lot of feeling) 9. Danza Apache 10. Hizo una donación para el colegio nuevo (made a donation for the new school).

Los deportes

Todos somos Guerreros

A 1. special promotions for the Guerreros' baseball games in July and August 2. Thursdays, July 19 and August 2; Any gentleman who buys a ticket for himself can bring in a lady free of charge, provided she wears the team colors. 3. red, white, and black 4. 50 pesos 5. Tato/He sponsors games and contests. 6. Three adults get a discounted ticket plus a "torta" and a drink each. 7. Two can go to Saturday's game for the price of one. 8. Children under twelve are admitted free on July 20 and August 3. No; they must be accompanied by a paying adult. 9. Family Sunday 10. San José and Pasadena 11. Estadio Central

Noticias de béisbol

A 1. batting average 2. a win 3. his compatriot (fellow countryman) 4. home run 5. designated hitter 6. an error 7. an inning

B 1. la segunda base, la tercera base 2. el segunda base, el tercera base

C 1. los Cachorros 2. los Azulejos 3. los Rojos 4. los Medias Rojas 5. los Tigres 6. los Astros 7. los Cardenales 8. los Yanquis 9. los Padres 10. los Medias Blancas 11. los Indios 12. los Vigilantes

D 1. a fence-flyer 2. a forest-guard 3. out-of-the-park home run, outfielder

E 1. el bate, batear, el bateador 2. lanzar 3. la carrera, correr

F el tablazo, el batazo

G 1. g 2. k 3. i 4. f 5. h 6. b 7. c 8. d 9. a 10. e 11. j 12. o 13. p 14. l 15. m 16. n 17. q 18. s 19. r 20. v 21. w 22. t 23. u

Edgar Martínez

A *Nouns:* 1. imparable 2. bateador 3. béisbol 4. fanático 5. serie divisional 6. un doble 7. la primera base 8. el bate 9. unas impulsadas 10. bases por bolas *Verbs:* 1. impulsar 2. manejar 3. batear 4. liderar

B 1. hitter 2. winning 3. lifetime 4. season 5. wrecker

Javier Quirós vuelve a la pista

A 1. Costa Rica 2. race-car driving 3. the Daytona 24 Hours

B 1. made an outcry/was upset 2. racing team 3. spokesman 4. exceed 5. they will rotate 6. added 7. cooperation

C La familia jaló mucho, mas todo se acomodó. The family had a fit, but everything worked out. Este piloto habla con conocimiento de causa pues ganó Le Mans en tres ocasiones. This pilot speaks with authority, as he won the Le Mans three times.

D 1. romper, cabezas 2. puzzle

E 1. 4 years 2. AASCO 3. Andy Durduck, Craig Stanton 4. BMW-3, 8 cylinders, 480 hp 5. Jaime Peña 6. running, lifting weights, doing neck and leg exercises 7. yes 8. He has won the Daytona five times and the Le Mans three times.

Una hispana en la WNBA

A 1. Levys Torres 2. Colombia 3. basketball 4. Miami Sol 5. only one

B 1. se inclinó, inclinarse 2. pensó, pensar 3. abordó, abordar 4. invitó, invitar 5. accedió, acceder 6. comenzó, comenzar 7. ganó, ganar 8. ingresó, ingresar 9. promedió, promediar 10. se convirtió, convertirse

C 1. to be inclined 2. to think 3. to approach 4. to invite 5. to agree to 6. to begin 7. to win 8. to enter 9. to average 10. to become

D 1. Deambulaba por una calle. (She was walking down the street.) 2. Entrenaba un equipo. (He was training a team.)

E 1. 15 2. in Barranquilla 3. 1.93 meters tall 4. the South American Tournament, in 1997 5. Florida State University, 1999 6. 10.8 points and 10 rebounds per game 7. April 25, 2001 8. one year

Nicolás Lapentti

A 1. forehand, short(s), web page, set, net 2. ranqueado

B 1. h 2. e 3. a 4. i 5. b 6. d 7. j 8. f 9. c 10. g

C 1. sensible 2. emocionante 3. impulsiva

D 1. achievement 2. struggle 3. attainment 4. reinforcement 5. support

E 1. late 2. trademark cap 3. the Open 4. tired 5. fans 6. clay courts 7. I thank him 8. superstition 9. locker room

F 1. a. also b. also c. in addition (besides) 2. a. naturally b. of course 3. a. thinner and thinner b. stronger and stronger c. harder and harder

Fútbol centroamericano

A *Sustantivos:* 1. liga 2. estrella 3. región 4. parte 5. continente 6. éxodo 7. economía 8. familia 9. negocio *Adjetivos:* 1. distinta 2. raro 3. europeo 4. regional *Verbos:* 1. exportar 2. militar 3. triunfar 4. colaborar 5. practicar

B 1. for quite a while 2. ever since it began

C 1. We're finally at the stadium. Let's watch the game. 2. "El Pescadito" isn't from El Salvador; he's from Guatemala. 3. The players are not only good, they're also less expensive. 4. His son has been a professional soccer player for three years now. 5. He spends the whole day talking about soccer. After all, it's his job.

Tres historias

A 1. 1946 2. el uruguayo Nacional, el argentino San Lorenzo 3. los del Nacional 4. San Lorenzo 5. meter goles 6. Martino 7. corrió rápido a la derecha 8. se echaron sobre Pontoni 9. Martino

B 1. 1961 2. Real Madrid, Atlético de Madrid 3. Ferenc Puskas, Real Madrid 4. húngaro 5. porque no había pitado 6. Puskas hizo un gol idéntico al primero.

C 1. 1973, Buenos Aires 2. los Argentinos Juniors, River Plate 3. 10 4. 100 5. "El Veneno" 6. Diego Maradona 7. técnico industrial

El cine y el teatro

Películas en cartel

A 1. *La vida prometida, Tarzán* 2. *Pásate a la pasta,* Italia 3. *La vida prometida, Tarzán* 4. *El mar* 5. Estrella, Estación de Chamartín La Dehesa 6. at 7:30 P.M. 7. *La vida prometida, Todo sobre mi madre* 8. the Goyas, the Cannes' awards, the Golden Globe 9. sound track, *Tarzán* 10. *La vida prometida*—World War II, *El mar*—the Spanish Civil War

B *Sustantivos:* 1. drama 2. comedy 3. effect 4. triumph 5. misery 6. myth 7. history 8. island 9. horror 10. spiral 11. innocence 12. humility 13. director 14. editor 15. feminist 16. gorilla 17. animal 18. adaptation 19. relation 20. condition 21. production 22. lesson *Adjetivos:* 1. difficult 2. radical 3. respective 4. honest 5. modest 6. permanent 7. literary 8. frequented 9. human 10. capable 11. magnificent 12. sophisticated 13. passionate 14. recognized 15. nominated *Verbos:* 1. to succumb 2. to hide 3. to serve 4. to convert 5. to dominate 6. to discover 7. to relate 8. to generate

C 1. salida 2. suceso 3. éxito

Solas

A 1. convivir, to live together 2. malvivir, to live in bad conditions

B 1. the encounter (meeting) 2. failure to meet up, mix-up

C the hardness or toughness

D 1. la hermosura 2. la gordura 3. sweetness

E 1. la soledad 2. la ciudad 3. la dignidad 4. la calidad 5. la dificultad 6. -dad 7. feminine

F 1. la dirección 2. la televisión 3. la mención 4. la canción 5. la producción 6. -ción/-sión 7. feminine

G 1. ganar, ganador/ganadora 2. perder, perdedor/perdedora 3. iluminar, iluminador/iluminadora 4. dirigir, director/directora 5. -or/-ora

H 1. tiene vergüenza 2. está embarazada

I 1. see themselves 2. hermit 3. is determined 4. go through 5. environment 6. huge 7. debut 8. dubbing 9. plays the part 10. medium-length film

Todo sobre mi madre

A *Sustantivos:* 1. sinopsis 2. refrán 3. el presente 4. el futuro 5. hospital 6. línea 7. nota 8. la impresión 9. en memoria de *Adjetivos*: 1. titulada 2. biológico *Verbos:* 1. recibió 2. se confunden 3. de que no se separa 4. encontrar 5. lo abandonó 6. resultar *Adverbios:* 1. totalmente

B 1. abandona 2. oscuridad 3. abandonar, embarazada 4. última 5. a continuación 6. tiene vergüenza 7. una continuación

C 1. movie 2. woman 3. dry 4. piece 5. take away from 6. simple

D 1. even though he didn't know him 2. before you were born 3. before he changed his name

E 1. Oscar for best foreign film 2. Manuela 3. Esteban 4. Esteban 5. Barcelona 6. no 7. *Answers will vary.*

Carlos Saura

A *Sustantivos:* 1. director 2. corto 3. vanguardia 4. trilogía 5. producción 6. duración 7. la actuación 8. grupo 9. sentimiento 10. música 11. interpretación 12. recurso *Adjetivos:* 1. extraordinario 2. glamoroso 3. refinado 4. espontáneo 5. impresionante 6. teatral 7. musical

8. en blanco *Verbos:* 1. mover 2. incluir 3. comenzar 4. expresar 5. capturar 6. representar 7. combinar *Adverbio:* 1. rápidamente

B 1. lo clásico 2. lo popular 3. lo experimental 4. lo narrativo 5. lo pantomímico

C 1. f 2. g 3. a 4. e 5. d 6. b 7. c

D desde el atardecer hasta el amanecer

Yo nunca quise ser escritor

A 1. la salida 2. los sucesos 3. El éxito

B crítico, Criticó, la crítica, la crítica

C Se estrenó la película en Chile el año pasado.

D 1. The movie will be shown next week. 2. The movie was shown last week. 3. The movie was filmed in Lima.

E 1. He abandoned reporting and writing reviews in order to devote his time to writing. 2. That's why I got away from writing reviews. 3. And then I realized that it was just a reviewer's opinion.

F 1. It was when I was finishing school that it occurred to me to write. 2. Don't ever forget that there will always be somebody who will read you (your work).

G 1. during 2. after 3. during

H 1. overdose 2. rewind it 3. bad news (a shame) 4. mood I'm in

I 1. periodismo amarillo 2. artista-artista

J 1. Chile, writer 2. movie critic, writer 3. *El Mercurio* 4. de Palma, Truffaut, Spielberg, Woody Allen 5. arty films for intellectual snobs 6. It wasn't perfect, but he's satisfied.

Fundación Arlequín Teatro

A 1. "Willy y nosotros," "Abran cancha que aquí viene Don Quijote de la Mancha," "El médico a palos" 2. "Abran cancha que aquí viene Don Quijote de la Mancha" 3. "Willy y nosotros," "Abran cancha...," "El médico a palos," "La casa de Bernarda Alba" 4. "Willy y nosotros," "Abran cancha..." 5. "El médico a palos" 6. "Abran cancha...," "El médico a palos" 7. At least since 1983 8. José Luis Ardissone 9. Jorge Krauch 10. "La tierra sin mal," Augusto Roa Bastos

B 1. interspersed/interwoven/intertwined/combined 2. most important 3. cast 4. comic/carnival-like/burlesque, believers (straight/serious/real) 5. the curtain

El fabricante de deudas

A 1. Obedot and Godofreda 2. badly 3. no 4. giving him all of her savings

B 1. llama 2. ruégale 3. pon 4. corre 5. no olvides 6. arréglate 7. anda 8. diles 9. insiste 10. vuela 11. acude 12. abre 13. inspírales 14. dales

C 1. the order 2. the receipt 3. sols (currency in Perú)

D dinero contante y sonante

E 1. intimidated 2. to cover up 3. open doors, make possible 4. delicious dishes 5. avarice, greed 6. business partner 7. never

F He is probably very fat.

G 1. Es un hombre que vive como rico, pero no tiene dinero. (He's a man who lives like a rich man, but has no money.) 2. Muy mal (very badly) 3. que llame al señor Obeso y que no olvide el whisky y el champán (to call Mr. Obeso and not to forget the whisky and the champagne) 4. que vaya a recoger el pedido de la señora (to pick up his wife's order) 5. el chofer (the chauffeur) 6. van a hacer una cena elegante (they are having a fancy dinner) 7. el Marqués de Rondavieja 8. siete (seven) 9. a otras tiendas (to other stores) 10. Godofreda 11. robarle los ahorros a Godofreda (rob Godofreda of her savings) 12. aparentemente, sí (apparently, yes)

El arte

Museos

A 1. El Museo Histórico de la República, Museo del Hombre 2. Sala Bancatlán 3. Museo Nacional Villaroy, Sala Bancatlán, El Museo de Antropología e Historia de San Pedro Sula 4. El Museo de Antropología e Historia de San Pedro Sula 5. Sala Bancatlán

El arco iris

A 1. azul 2. verde 3. naranja 4. violeta 5. magenta 6. ocre 7. café 8. rosa 9. gris 10. amarillo 11. blanco 12. negro 13. rojo

El muralismo mexicano

A 1. Mexico's 2. in the late 1920s

B *Nouns:* 1. artista 2. círculo 3. color 4. costumbre 5. década 6. disposición 7. forma 8. gobierno 9. historia 10. idea 11. momento 12. movimiento 13. pintor 14. revolución 15. espacio 16. valor
Adjectives: 1. mural 2. público 3. entusiasmados 4. social 5. común 6. ultraintelectual 7. aristocrático

C 1. vitalidad 2. originalidad 3. creatividad 4. genialidad

D 1. el/la socialista 2. el/la monumentalista 3. el/la cubista 4. el surrealismo 5. el/la expresionista 6. el futurismo 7. el/la impresionista 8. el/la modernista

E 1. decidió 2. declararon 3. captured 4. propagated 5. expressed

F 1. began (was born) 2. brought 3. devoted themselves 4. property 5. objective (goal) 6. emphasize, give greater importance to 7. struggle

G 1. to unite the people by reminding them of the glories of the Revolution 2. Diego Rivera, José Clemente Orozco, David Alfaro Siqueiros 3. art that belongs to the people (art for the public) 4. their simplicity, vitality, and originality in capturing the flavor and history of Mexico

Frida Kahlo

A 1. Mexican 2. Diego Rivera

B 1. introspectivamente 2. sociablemente 3. felizmente 4. psicológicamente 5. histéricamente 6. cariñosamente 7. terriblemente 8. físicamente 9. mentalmente 10. profundamente 11. preponderantemente 12. intensamente

C 1. traumatizada 2. malformada 3. aislado 4. heridos 5. fracturado 6. dislocado 7. divorciada 8. rota

D 1. sensible 2. sensato 3. secuestrar 4. aislada

E 1. July 6, 1907 2. Her father's last name is Hungarian and her mother's is Spanish. 3. sensitive and introspective 4. poliomyelitis and an accident 5. She wore pants when she was young; later, she wore long Mexican skirts. 6. both wonderful and torturous 7. its intensely human expression

Pablo Picasso

A 1. a painter and sculptor 2. Spain

B 1. *Answers will vary.* 2. *Answers will vary.*

C 1. drawings, paintings, sculptures, lithographs 2. He created over 20,000 works of art. 3. clarity, craziness, grace, passion, passionate anger, arbitrariness, mockery 4. his huge, happy heart

Salvador Dalí

A 1. a painter 2. Spain

B His themes vary from the erotic to the religious.

C the ability to paint extraordinary scenes in the middle of an empty desert, the ability to paint with patience a pear surrounded by the great disturbances of history

D He gives his wife names that remind him of the shape of her face and the color of her skin. He gives her pet names that repeat sounds and syllables. Yes.

E 1. Cataluña 2. his surrealism painted with realistic detail 3. cinematography, commercial projects 4. a big smile

Fernando Botero

A 1. a. breaking out in b. to begin to do something 2. a. he raises b. to raise 3. filling 4. hole

B 1. no resiste/no aguanta/no soporta 2. apoya 3. no se resiste a 4. se resiste a aceptar/se niega a aceptar/no quiere aceptar

C 1. Botero lleva mucho tiempo viviendo fuera de su país. 2. Lleva veinte años pintando. 3. Llevamos treinta minutos (media hora) esperándote.

D 1. a pesar de 2. sino 3. sino 4. a pesar de 5. a pesar de

E 1. juega el papel 2. juega un papel 3. escribir un trabajo

F 1. Colombia 2. la gordura 3. el trabajo 4. pobre 5. José Clemente Orozco 6. realidad imaginaria

A la manera de Frida Kahlo

A 1. y una lágrima me ablandaba la silla 2. y se me perdía el mundo 3. o daba vueltas la página 4. o solamente estaba en medio de una habitación inmaculada 5. y la infancia se hundía con camisones sin florcitas y pies rosados 6. mientras mis riñones soltaban charcos de sangre 7. y afuera, en la ventana la plaza aparecía repleta de palomas 8. A veces yo perdía los anteojos

B 1. b 2. g 3. f 4. a 5. e 6. d 7. h 8. c

C 1. The other children were playing a game. 2. her ABCs

Graffiti

A 1. el hermano 2. cuatro 3. lápices de cera 4. Jackson Pollock 5. seguir el rastro del misterio, de lo imposible 6. tres días y tres noches, y la gran parte del cuarto día

La familia

El árbol familiar

A 1. mother-in-law 2. brother-in-law 3. nephew 4. son-in-law 5. granddaughter 6. daughter-in-law 7. brothers (siblings) 8. aunt and uncle 9. parents 10. children (sons and daughters)

B 1. tío 2. tía 3. primos 4. cuñada 5. sobrinos 6. la abuela 7. la suegra

C 1. González 2. María 3. García 4. González 5. yes 6. *Answers will vary.*

La celebración del matrimonio

A 1. Elena and Ricardo 2. religious 3. yes 4. yes

B 1. la concentración 2. celebrar 3. la renunciación 4. conservar 5. separar 6. la reunión

C 1. cuanto puedan 2. nos separe

D 1. la riqueza, rico 2. la pobreza, pobre

E 1. others 2. witnesses 3. support 4. from today on (from this day forward)

F 1. tanto en tiempo de enfermedad como de salud 2. Puesto que Elena y Ricardo se han dado el uno al otro por medio de votos solemnes, con la unión de las manos y con la entrega y recepción de anillos, yo los declaro esposo y esposa, en el Nombre del Padre, y del Hijo y del Espíritu Santo.

A mi hija Flor de María

A 1. Carlomagno Araya 2. his daughter

B 1. Flor de María 2. one year old 3. walk 4. a doll and a piece of candy 5. adores her

La familia: un invento maravilloso

A 1. yes 2. yes

B 1. miss 2. oppresses or haunts 3. oppressive 4. miss 5. I longed for

C 1. things don't smile at you 2. my mother was like a general 3. Hotel Mom 4. a club of applause (fan club)

D 1. a place of comfort, maybe taken for granted and slightly oppressive 2. an appreciation of and longing for that comfort, and a desire to re-create it 3. an understanding that history will repeat itself, but is hopefully slightly better with each generation

La familia de Marcela

A 1. no, sino más bien 2. mucho más 3. para que 4. pues 5. por 6. pues 7. claro 8. ya sea 9. pues

B 1. usually 2. attainments or achievements, losses 3. again (history repeats itself again) 4. at the same time or also 5. suitors 6. a rib

C 1. sensata 2. sensible

D *Answers will vary.*

Un padre

A 1. Mi papá no tenía dinero 2. Había una tienda en la esquina de su casa 3. la sopa era un platillo que nos iba a ayudar a ver mejor 4. Mientras tomábamos la sopa 5. los ojos nos miraban constantemente 6. se trataba de una broma

B 1. Una Navidad le pedimos un tren eléctrico. 2. Recogió latas de la basura, 3. las llevó a su estudio, 4. y nos hizo unas armaduras y unas espadas. 5. Mi papá fue a una tienda de prótesis 6. y compró tres pares de ojos de cristal. 7. Preparó una sopa de cenar y nos dijo... 8. le echó los ojos 9. Él jamás soltó ni siquiera una sonrisa 10. Fue una cena aterradora.

C 1. Era un hombre creativo. 2. Vivía en Nueva York. 3. Lo visitaban sus hijos durante sus vacaciones. 4. Querían un tren eléctrico. 5. Les regaló unas armaduras y unas espadas. 6. Sí, fueron los mejores regalos. 7. Puso ojos de cristal en la sopa. 8. Son muy buenas memorias.

Los abuelos

A 1. fourth graders 2. They are to ask their grandparents to teach them their childhood games. The children, in turn, will have to teach their grandparents the games they play.

B 1. c, e 2. b, g 3. a 4. f 5. h 6. d

C 1. pelota 2. travesuras 3. ollas, trastos 4. adivinanza 5. agarrar 6. olla 7. trasto

D 1. choose, count, hide; Hide and Seek 2. circle 3. jacks, grab; Jacks 4. jump rope; Jump Rope 5. spinning top; The Spinning Top

E 1. Hablan con sus abuelos sobre cuando eran niños. (They interview them about when they were young.) 2. escondidas (hide and seek), la gallina ciega (the blind hen), la Rueda de San Miguel, el trompo (the spinning top), canicas (marbles), la cuerda (jump rope), la matatena (jacks), muñecas de trapo (rag dolls), ollas y trastecitos (pots and utensils) 3. Nintendo, básquetbol, fútbol, Barbis 4. *Answers will vary.* 5. *Answers will vary.*

Cuentos

A 1. Él y Maribel cenan juntos. 2. a. todo lo bueno b. lo bueno real o imaginario

B 1. event/occasion 2. passing 3. it lacks 4. blush, show 5. knot

C *Story No. 8:* 1. his ex-wife 2. the day they separated 3. every year 4. each gives a monologue 5. no 6. a whole year *Story No. 10:* 7. the father 8. twenty years 9. to the place he came from 10. the grandmother 11. because she can't forgive him

El estilo de vida hoy

Terra Venezuela

A 1. March 27, 2002 2. Semana Santa (Holy Week) 3. Francisco Fajardo 4. the best place to spend Semana Santa, the Oscars 5. Empleos 6. CDs by Franco De Vita 7. "Necesidad" 8. Umi 5, for learning to read 9. Fifa 2002 10. Invertía, Economía 11. Yes: Mall de Compras, Desarrollo de Tiendas Virtuales 12. Horóscopo, Horóscopo Semanal, Tarot, W. Mercado 13. Login and Password 14. Hacer clic en Contáctenos

Mi PC

A 1. his girlfriend 2. in his computer 3. her kisses 4. her personality 5. the mouse 6. the mouse 7. her eyes 8. her body 9. her smile and her hair 10. a disk with a little bit of his affection 11. a limousine, a Hugo Boss vest, Cindy Crawford in Berlin, a palace with pagodas, a Burger King, not even a Miró drawing 12. her affection at night

Cristina

A *Nouns:* 1. momento 2. proceso 3. reflexión 4. análisis 5. orientación 6. repercusión 7. decisión 8. acción 9. gloria 10. fama 11. situación 12. consideración 13. alternativa 14. experiencia 15. comprensión
Adjectives: 1. formidable 2. posible 3. famoso 4. relativo
Verbs: 1. organizar 2. comunicar 3. preparar 4. garantizar

B 1. feminine 2. la organización 3. la comunicación 4. la preparación

C 1. corriente 2. actual 3. verdadera

D 1. se 2. le

E 1. cambié 2. conté 3. logré 4. preparé 5. tomé

F 1. comencé 2. expliqué 3. llegué 4. garanticé 5. organicé 6. comuniqué 7. alcancé 8. dediqué 9. tracé

G 1. hice 2. tuve

H 1. in the long run 2. will 3. happiness 4. bump 5. mud 6. fear 7. goal 8. to be worthwhile

I 1. no 2. the will 3. young people 4. being rich, famous, having a relative degree of happiness 5. It's full of bumps, thorns, mud, and fear. 6. no 7. yes 8. learn and change 9. her experience, understanding, and love

Oscar de la Renta

A 1. dibujante, illustrator 2. diseñador, designer 3. costurero, fashion designer

B 1. nacimiento, birth 2. sentimiento, feeling 3. conocimiento, knowledge 4. reconocimiento, recognition

C 1. prize/award 2. he left 3. popular/coveted 4. high fashion/couture 5. label 6. has grown

D 1. the Dominican Republic 2. He's a fashion designer. 3. la Academia de San Fernando in Madrid, Spain 4. Balenciaga, Lanvin, Elizabeth Arden, Pierre Balmain 5. Signature 6. Pour Lui, Oscar for Men 7. He has built schools.

Carolina Herrera, qué mujer

A 1. She's a fashion designer. 2. New York 3. women's clothing, perfume, bridal gowns

B 1. ha triunfado 2. ha sabido 3. siempre ha sido 4. no ha cambiado 5. ¿ha decidido...? 6. ha influido 7. he hecho 8. siempre ha habido

C 1. perfectamente 2. lentamente 3. inexorablemente 4. rotundamente 5. ciegamente 6. profesionalmente 7. claramente 8. exactamente

D 1. quite an empire 2. every designer 3. especially 4. for example 5. more informal every day 6. you couldn't even imagine 7. then

E 1. distance/get away from 2. launches/introduces 3. surround 4. I don't consider it 5. predict 6. It's not a good idea for me 7. to find out 8. at the end of

F 1. elegance without excess 2. no 3. It's a fashion center, and the Europeans want to be a part of it. 4. no 5. every three months 6. wear them with their own personal style 7. perfume 8. a little innocent, without too much makeup

Edward James Olmos

A 1. Edward James Olmos 2. the United States 3. movie and television actor 4. indigenous communities in El Salvador 5. as a representative of UNICEF 6. yes

B 1. indigenous communities 2. more than thirteen years 3. They give the children the self-esteem they need in order to be, to grow, and to do everything in life. 4. There is only one: the human race. 5. his mother 6. a school to learn the native language 7. the need for native land ownership, the desire to teach indigenous language and customs to the younger generation, health and nutrition problems faced by the children 8. hurricane Mitch 9. doing his best every day 10. at the Radio Station "Atunal" 11. that he would report what he found to UNICEF, and that he would return to El Salvador 12. Hispanic culture

Un día insólito

A 1. He is a lawyer. 2. at the office 3. Tina 4. stressed out 5. his sister

B 1. avoid 2. trash heap 3. crystal Christmas decorations (bells and reindeer) 4. junk 5. leaving for a trip 6. take the responsibility for

C 1. una montaña de papeles (a mountain of papers) 2. el desorden crecía a su alrededor amenazando con devorarlo (the disorder grew around him, threatening to eat him up)

D parece un basural (it looks like a trash heap)

E 1. el Sr. Reeves (Mr. Reeves) 2. desordenada (messy) 3. muy nervioso (stressed out) 4. su secretaria (his secretary) 5. hacer una declaración, ir a los tribunales (make a declaration, go to court) 6. su hermana (his sister) 7. su hijo (his son) 8. sus propios hijos y su madre (her own children and her mother)

La historia y la política

Cronología

A 1. the Mayan 2. almost 800 years 3. the conquest of Granada, the discovery of the Americas 4. Peru, 300 years 5. Carlos V 6. Santo Domingo 7. 1539 8. four 9. Paraguay, Mexico 10. the war with Napoleon 11. California, Utah, Nevada, and parts of Arizona, New Mexico, Colorado, and Wyoming 12. the French Emperor of Mexico 13. Alfonso XII 14. as an outcome of the 1898 war with Spain 15. Panama and Cuba became independent, Mexico had a cultural revolution, the Panama Canal opened 16. the dictatorship of General Francisco Franco 17. 18 years 18. Cuba, Nicaragua, Chile 19. the reestablishment of democracy, a new constitution 20. the Central American Common Market, the Mercosur Treaty, the North American Free Trade Agreement, the ALC between Mexico and the European Union

Celebrando la independencia

A *Nouns:* 1. autoridad 2. gabinete 3. capital 4. celebración 5. costumbre 6. documento 7. dominio 8. historia 9. honor 10. independencia 11. momento 12. sesión 13. territorio 14. tradición *Adjectives:* 1. glorioso 2. importante 3. significativo 4. típico *Verbs:* 1. celebrar 2. liberar

B 1. personajes 2. tipo 3. reputación 4. personaje

C 1. pride, celebrates, achieved (won) 2. dancers 3. I swear 4. They feel 5. sign 6. attend 7. mass 8. school children, parade 9. get together

D 1. Alto Peru is known today as Bolivia. 2. The Casa de la Independencia is the place where the document was signed. 3. A session of honor is held. 4. The altar is decorated with images of Bolívar and Sucre. 5. Friends and family members get together in private homes. 6. Dancing is popular at parties.

E takes place

F 1. August 6 2. Alto Perú 3. La Paz 4. Simón Bolívar 5. in la Casa de la Independencia 6. the president, his cabinet members, and other important leaders 7. a Catholic Mass 8. with food and dancing

Ayuda humanitaria

A 1. Perú 2. Venezuela

B 1. was delivered 2. burned people 3. hurt 4. we brought 5. was received 6. the wounded are assisted

C 1. Lima, December 29 2. 280 3. 11 tons 4. by military plane 5. the Venezuelan Embassy, the National Civil Defense Institute 6. medicine, surgical equipment, special bedding for burn victims

El Canal de Panamá

A 1. advances 2. slide/slip, canal locks 3. sets of canal locks 4. job/task 5. emerged 6. cargo ship, crossing 7. stage/chapter 8. signed 9. handing over/delivering 10. toll 11. save, amount 12. weight/displacement of weight

B In Spanish, commas are used for decimals and periods are used to mark thousands.

C 1. Carlos V, 1524 2. He had directed the building of the Suez Canal, France 3. disease and financial problems 4. 1903, a treaty was signed with the United States giving it the authority to build a canal 5. *Ancón* 6. a treaty was signed assuring the return of the canal to Panama, el General Omar Torrijos Herrera, el presidente Jimmy Carter 7. 20 years 8. $29,000 9. $165,235.58, 36 cents

Puente binacional

A 1. Bolivia, Perú 2. a new bridge that links the two countries

B 1. inaugurarán 2. sustituirá 3. ingresará 4. se reunirán 5. analizarán 6. será 7. abordarán 8. pondrán en marcha 9. permitirá

C 1. Jorge Quiroga, Alejandro Toledo 2. Toledo 3. the construction of a bridge, January 27 4. the Corporación Andina de Fomento 5. better traffic flow and safety 6. development of southern Perú and western Bolivia, export of natural gas from Bolivia, an insurance plan for rural areas at the border of the two countries

La pacifista

A 1. Ana Teresa Bernal 2. determined fighter for peace 3. to achieve peace in Colombia

B 1. vio, ella 2. oyó, ella 3. se prometió, ella 4. tapizaron, los artistas 5. dieron a luz, los artistas 6. lideró, Ana Teresa 7. luchó, ese grupo 8. fueron; una cena, una vuelta a Colombia y cientos de foros 9. perdió, el movimiento 10. se transformó, el movimiento 11. votaron, 10 millones de colombianos 12. tuvo, esa bogotana (ella) 13. aprendió, ella 14. se casó, ella 15. se aburrió, ella 16. volvió, ella 17. se vinculó, ella 18. coqueteó, ella

C 1. desaparecía bajo las llamas 2. parecía más 3. iban, leía 4. repartía 5. enfurecía 6. enfilaban

D 1. trabajen 2. enseñe 3. viva

E 1. trabajaran 2. enseñara

F 1. apostó 2. aporte, impulsar 3. volantes 4. La convivencia 5. el volante 6. volantes

G 1. begged 2. struggle 3. covered 4. gave birth 5. they founded 6. flames, rescued 7. revive 8. baton 9. leadership 10. grabbed the reins 11. to take charge 12. start over 13. start over 14. gets discouraged 15. use the cape to confuse the bull 16. confront and win over 17. resorting 18. resorting

H 1. la Semana por la Paz 2. el Movimiento por la Vida, la Redepaz, el Mandato Ciudadano por la Paz, la Juco, Firmes 3. del 8 hasta el 13 de septiembre 4. hablan de la paz, piensan en cómo hacerles resistencia a los guerreros, asumen iniciativas ciudadanas para coger las riendas del país 5. la irreverencia, la pasión por lo bello y la forma de cambiar las costumbres sin recurrir a la violencia 6. delegada en el Comité temático de los diálogos con las FARC 7. la Red de Iniciativas Ciudadanas por la Paz y contra la Guerra 8. que sean capaces de cambiar el país sin matarse

Una conversación entre marido y mujer

A 1. Cásate. 2. Quédate tranquila. (tú) / Quedáte tranquila. (vos)

B 1. No abandones a los pobres. 2. No te hagas el gracioso. 3. No dejes que me olviden.

C 1. Todos estos que andan por aquí lamiéndote los zapatos. 2. Me paso el día contestando las cartas que te mandan a vos.

D 1. Chinita 2. más de tres mil cartas 3. una beca, ajuares de novia, juegos de dormitorio 4. muy enferma 5. que no abandone a los pobres 6. los pobres 7. que no deje que la gente la olvide 8. Evita y Juan Perón

Acknowledgments

p. 3
Guía para la buena alimentación: Courtesy of National Dairy Council®.

pp. 18–19
From *Las fiestas de Frida y Diego* by Guadalupe Rivera and Marie-Pierre Colle, copyright © 1994 by Guadalupe Rivera and Marie-Pierre Colle. Used by permission of Clarkson Potter/Publishers, a division of Random House, Inc.

pp. 22–23
From *Como agua para chocolate* by Laura Esquivel, copyright © 1989 by Laura Esquivel. Used by permission of Doubleday, a division of Random House, Inc.

p. 45
From *Cuando era puertorriqueña* by Esmeralda Santiago. Used by permission of Vintage Books, a division of Random House, Inc.

p. 58
Reprinted from *Latino Baseball Magazine*/R. Paniagua Inc.

p. 64
From *Acción Deportiva,* 14 de agosto de 2001.

p. 71
From Renán Cardona, in *Acción Deportiva,* 14 de agosto de 2001.

p. 97 and p. 214
Semana, 27 de agosto de 2001. Authority recognized exclusively to *Semana Magazine,* Colombia.

p. 169
From *¡Cristina!: Confidencias de una rubia* by Cristina Saralegui. Copyright © 1998 by Cristina Saralegui Enterprises, Inc. By permission of Warner Books, Inc.

p. 187
From *El plan infinito* by Isabel Allende.

p. 221
From *Santa Evita* by Tomás Eloy Martínez, copyright © 1996 by Alfred A. Knopf, Inc. Used by permission of Alfred A. Knopf, a division of Random House, Inc.